# Lighthouses
### of Liverpool Bay

# Lighthouses

## of Liverpool Bay

John and Diane Robinson

TEMPUS

First published 2007

Tempus Publishing Limited
The Mill, Brimscombe Port,
Stroud, Gloucestershire, GL5 2QG
www.tempus-publishing.com

British Library Cataloguing in Publication Data.
A catalogue record for this book is available from the British Library.

ISBN 978-07524-4209-0

Typesetting and origination by Tempus Publishing Limited
Printed in Great Britain

# CONTENTS

# Illustration Acknowledgements

Boumphrey, Ian 103
Bryson, Colonel G. 118, 123, 124
Cheshire & Chester Archives and Local Studies 63, 68 (top), 83
Davidson, A.S. 96
Denham, H.M. in *Sailing Directions from Point Lynas to Liverpool* 18, 32, 54, 106 (top left), 117, 130 (top), 138 (bottom left)
From the collection of the Royal Monuments Record of Wales: Howarth-Loomes Collection 157
*Illustrated London News* 128
Kingham, Paul 93 (right)
Leasowe Lighthouse Archive 36, 37
*Liverpool Daily Post* 39, 153
Liverpool Record Office, Liverpool Libraries 25 (top), 69, 101 (top), 113 (bottom)
Llandudno Archives 154
Merseyside Archaeological Society 47 (top)
Mersey Docks & Harbour Co. 21 (top), 57 (bottom), 58 (top), 64, 66, 68 (bottom), 137 (left and right), 138 (top), 138 (centre)
National Museums of Liverpool (Merseyside Maritime Museum) 120, 125, 126
Sefton Library Service 122
Trinity House 158, 170
Wallasey Reference Library 27, 84, 89
Warren, C.S. 164
Williamson Art Gallery & Museum, Birkenhead; Wirral Museums Service 43 (top), 47 (bottom), 57 (top), 91
Young, D. & M. 70 (top), 73, 76 (top), 78 (top), 80 (top)
www.mersey-gateway.org (3/6/05) 113 (top)
www.pol.ac.uk (13/1/04) 45 (bottom)
www.terrypepper.com/lights (21/5/06) 156

# Acknowledgements

In researching this book we have had the help of many libraries, record offices and archives. Our main effort has been concentrated at the Merseyside Maritime Museum archive, where the staff have been most helpful; especially John Moore, assistant curator, who is a fund of knowledge and knows where to find everything. Liverpool Record Office staff were kind and efficient, and we made great use of their extensive archive and facilities. The Liverpool Nautical Research Society has given us generous and willing advice. The Williamson Art Gallery, Birkenhead, has a wonderful collection of Victorian pictures of local lighthouses and we are grateful to Colin Simpson who has allowed us to reproduce them in our book.

Our local reference libraries have shown great patience, especially Jenny Done at Wallasey library and Pauline Black at Birkenhead Central. The librarians at Crosby, Formby and Southport were also most helpful. Further afield, we must offer our thanks to the staff at the Cheshire and Chester archives, Hawarden, Llandudno and Llangefni reference libraries and archives, as well as the library of the University of Wales, at Bangor. Our travels also took us to The National Archive, where the workforce is efficient and knowledgeable. Trinity House were very hospitable, allowing us the use of their library.

There are many individuals to whom we are indebted; in particular Colonel G. Bryson for his kindness and generous help. His collection of pictures and his personal knowledge were especially appreciated. Charlie Warren, the owner of Hoylake upper lighthouse, gave us and members of the Association of Lighthouse Keepers a warm welcome to his fascinating home. Fiona and Ray Kilpatrick of Great Ormes Head lighthouse were charming hosts in their remarkable guest-house and freely provided us with information and access for photography. Doug Darroch, of Fort Perch Rock, gave up an afternoon so we could have a memorable visit to New Brighton lighthouse. He provided much needed moral and physical support to enable Diane to climb the dreaded vertical ladder. We must also thank Ian Abernethy for valuable information on his lighthouse ancestor. Derek Young generously allowed us to use several pictures from his collection. Local historians Jim O'Neil and Joy Hockey gave us the benefit of their expertise.

The enthusiasm of the Association of Lighthouse Keepers provided us with the impetus to explore the lighthouses at New Brighton and Hoylake on a lovely weekend in excellent company.

With special thanks to Gerry Douglas-Sherwood, an ex-Principal Keeper with Trinity House, who sorted out our technical terms, and Jim Rodgers, who checked for spelling and punctuation errors.

Without the Friends of Leasowe Lighthouse this book would not have been written. Their commitment to the restoration has ensured that the old lighthouse has become part of our local heritage. Many members of the committee have been there since its inception in 1989, including the chairman Eric Johnson, who has played a pivotal role. They, together with the Rangers, have worked tirelessly to raise the necessary funds to renovate the fabric of the building.

# Preface

The Lighthouses of Liverpool Bay featured in this book were Liverpool's own lighthouses. Although Trinity House has, since Elizabethan times, been the general lighthouse authority for England and Wales, the Channel Islands and Gibraltar, Liverpool's lighthouses were built and administered by the Mersey Docks & Harbour Board (MDHB) and its predecessor, the Dock Trust. They were operational, as manned lighthouses, from about the mid-eighteenth to the early twentieth century.

Liverpool's iconic waterfront with the Mersey Docks & Harbour Board's building on the right.

Unless otherwise stated, all quotations are from the minutes of the committees and sub-committees of the MDHB and its predecessor. The terminology in these quotations is that of the MDHB, but in the narrative we have used the language of Trinity House to describe the technical details of lighthouses.

The story of Liverpool's lighthouses and the men and women who kept the lights are the subject of this book.

# Introduction

*The lighthouse lifts its massive masonry,*
*A pillar of fire by night,*
*Of cloud by day.*

Henry Wadsworth Longfellow, The Lighthouse.

Chester had been a great seaport from Roman times, but by 1550 the steady accumulation of silt had become a serious problem. Within another half century the port could no longer berth larger vessels. Its shipping trade was then carried on from small anchorages and quays along the Dee estuary; Burton Point, Parkgate, Dawpool and the Hoyle Lake.

## A SMALL HARBOUR

Liverpool was, until the middle of the seventeenth century, not as important a port as Chester. With Chester's demise, coupled with increased output from the developing industries in Lancashire and West Yorkshire,[1] Liverpool's traders and merchants set about turning the fishing harbour into an independent seaport. Their efforts were rewarded in 1660, when the port was first recognised by the Surveyor General of Customs to be 'distinct and absolute, of its selfe'.[2] But the estuary on which Liverpool stands has a ferociously swift tidal flow and is exposed to the prevailing wind and waves of the Irish Sea. Small vessels had to settle onto the beach while the tide was out. Larger ships discharged their cargoes in the deep, sheltered water of Hoyle Lake, some ten miles distant.

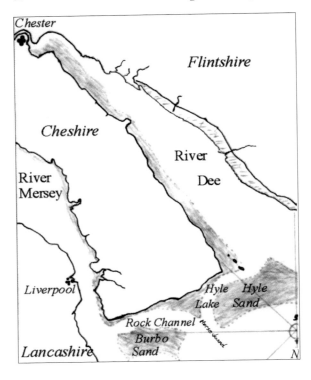

*Left:* This map is based on Grenville Collins's 1689 Chart of the Dee Estuary.

*Below:* Liverpool's Ancient Town and Harbour as depicted in Thomas Baines's *History of Liverpool*.

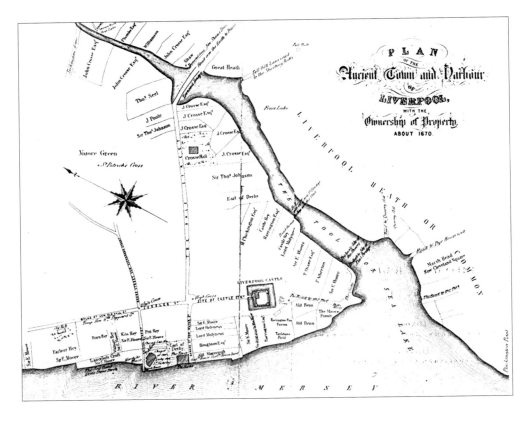

Liverpool's town map of 1670 shows the entrance to a tidal creek that opened into the Mersey estuary. The creek ran down the route of the present Whitechapel and Paradise Street. On the site of Canning Place it broadened out into a tidal basin known as 'The Pool'.

The port made steady progress in its early years. Then, with the passing of the first Liverpool Dock Act of 1708, the mayor, aldermen, bailiffs and common council were appointed members of the new Dock Trust.[3] A hundred years later, in celebrating the successful efforts of their forebears, the trustees of 1810 looked back at what had been achieved:

> It is not more than a century since Liverpool little exceeded the size of an ordinary fishing town. The number of its inhabitants in the year 1700 was about three thousand. The spirit of commercial enterprise however seems to have been very great, for in the year 1714, the Old Dock was constructed, which except Greenland Dock on the River Thames, was the first wet dock that was constructed in the island of Great Britain. This dock though of small extent, covering only about three acres and a half with water, was a very great work for the inhabitants of this small town at the time it was constructed, and afforded great security for their shipping, for the rapidity of the tide in the Mersey is great, and the shore much exposed, which subjected vessels to damage when unprotected.

The original vision that led Thomas Steers to build the Old Dock was of a canal basin, which retained water behind huge gates when the tide went out. London's Greenland Dock, originally called the Howland Great Wet Dock, was probably the world's first wet dock, having been given royal assent in 1696.[4] After Liverpool's Old Dock had been built, more docks and piers were constructed on land reclaimed from the river. The map below shows the dock system in 1796 with the outline of the original coastline and creek superimposed over it.

## A Large Sea-Lake

The large sea-lake known as Hoyle Lake was just off the north coast of the Wirral, by the modern town of Hoylake. Even when the tide was fully out, the lake was half a mile wide with a depth of 30ft at one end and 15ft at the other. It curved around the landward side of a huge sandbank, called Hyle or Hoyle Sand, between Dove Point and Red Rocks.

During the first half of the eighteenth century Liverpool needed Hoyle Lake to supplement its growing dock system. Here, ships could unload part of their cargo onto flat-bottomed vessels until they were light enough to go into port, over the shallows. They could also take shelter during stormy weather, or while waiting for a favourable wind. William III took advantage of the Hoyle Lake when he assembled his fleet there in 1690, prior to taking his army across to Ireland.[5] The lake may have been used as a refuge by vessels for centuries, protected as it was by the great Hyle Sand. This was only completely covered at the top of a

*Left:* Map of
Liverpool from
*The Liverpool
Guide* of 1796 with
the old coastline
superimposed.

*Below:* From
Captain Grenville
Collins's chart of
1689 with Hoyle
Lake indicated by
the Authors.

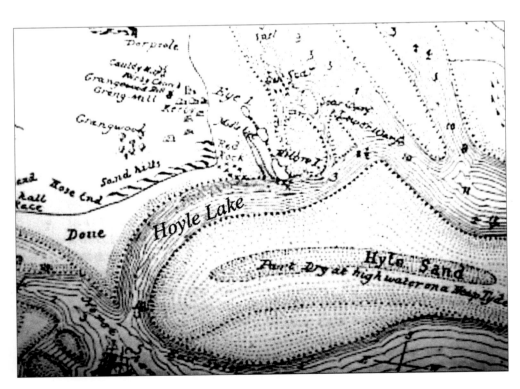

spring tide, when it could be 'seen as a ripple'.[6] The busy scene at Hoyle Lake was recorded by Celia Fiennes in her journal in 1698. Describing the view from Flint, across the Dee estuary, she wrote: '…here I went just in sight of High Lake where were many shipps rideing along that harbour'.[7] Yet it is a strange fact that this remarkable feature had almost completely disappeared by the mid-1800s.

## The First Lighthouses

In spite of protests by Trinity House, who had had almost exclusive control of the lighthouses of England and Wales since 1600, it became possible for individuals to obtain a parliamentary bill that permitted them to erect lighthouses and then collect revenue. This proved to be a highly profitable enterprise. In 1664 a gentleman named Reading began his attempt to obtain just such a bill for the building of a lighthouse on the Cheshire shore. Surprisingly perhaps, Liverpool's town councillors were very much against the idea. They argued that:

> …those lighthouses will be no benefit to our mariners, but a hurt, and expose them to those dangers if [they] trust to them, and also be a great and unnecessary burden and charge to them.[8]

The councillors were worried that wreckers may light fires to mislead mariners into running aground where the vessels would be plundered. Liverpool's councillors successfully intervened against the proposed lighthouse and in 1671 Mr Reading's bill failed.

Nearly a hundred years passed before attitudes changed. During that time many important changes had taken place:

1) The Pool stream was run into a culvert and the Pool itself was reclaimed, leaving space for Liverpool's first enclosed dock, which became known as the Old Dock. Opened in 1715 it was a great success, being able to hold eighty to a hundred ships.

2) In 1717 the marking out of the Formby Channel had begun. This produced a direct route into the Mersey for larger ships heading for Liverpool's new wet dock.

3) Liverpool's shipping trade had been increasing year on year, with vessels using Hoyle Lake and the Rock Channel. By 1683, some turning points and channels between the sandbanks had been marked with beacons, perches and buoys. In 1759 a floating light was moored to guide vessels into the Hoyle Lake.

4) Around 1725 the New Cut was dug, which canalised the Dee estuary towards Chester. This had a great effect on the distribution of the sand and silt within and beyond the Dee estuary.

By 1761 the town's merchants and ship owners were dismayed by the loss of ships, cargo and lives in the dangerous waters of Liverpool Bay. The main solution to this problem involved a plan to place four lighthouses on the Cheshire shore (known as the Cheshire Lights) that would guide ships into Hoyle Lake and then the Mersey estuary. To bring this about, a Bill was put before Parliament – the Liverpool Dock Act of 1762. Its wording stated the case clearly:

> …there being at present no lighthouses or other lights erected and set out, ships and vessels sailing to and from the said port and harbour of Liverpoole are frequently engaged in dark and tempestuous nights within the said banks and shoals and the navigation into and from the said port and harbour is very difficult, precarious and uncertain, whereby the lives and property of several of His Majesty's subjects have from time to time been lost, and are frequently endangered…

The Bill having succeeded, four lighthouses were erected in the form of two pairs of leading lights: the Sea Lights, at Mockbeggar and the Lake Lights, on the shore of Hoyle Lake. They were designed to lead ships safely into Hoyle Lake or onward, via the Rock Channel, to Liverpool.

The upper and lower Sea Lights were brick towers situated to the west of Leasowe Castle, then called Mockbeggar Hall. Alignment of these two lights, one directly above the other, gave the safe course along the Horse Channel. This ran, between Hoyle and Burbo banks, to the western entrance of the Rock Channel, and to the eastern entrance of Hoyle Lake.

The upper Lake Light was a brick tower and the lower Lake Light, on the beach, was a moveable wooden structure. They were positioned near the shore of the Hoyle Lake, where the town of Hoylake is now. Alignment of these two lights gave the course into Hoyle Lake from the Horse Channel.

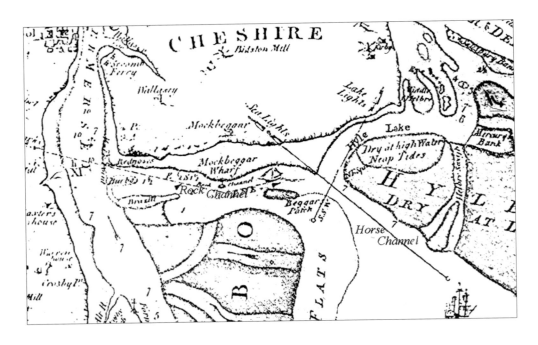

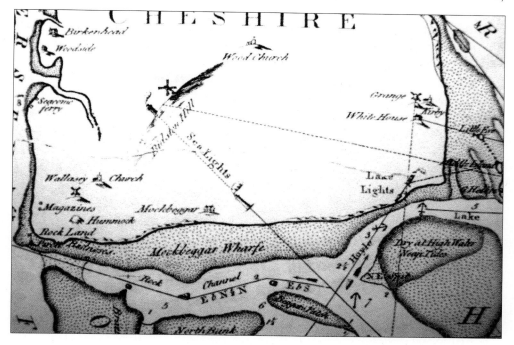

Burdett's Chart of the Harbour of Liverpool, 1771 (South at the top).

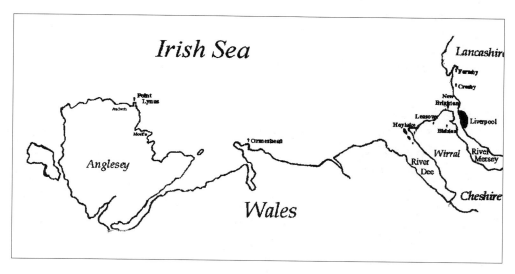

The positions of Liverpool's lighthouses.

*Opposite:* From Williamson's Chart of 1766 (South at the top).

After six or seven years, the lower Sea Light, at Leasowe, collapsed into the sea. It was replaced in 1771 by a lighthouse sited on Bidston Hill. This became the new upper Sea Light and the original upper Sea Light (the one standing at Leasowe to this day) then became the *lower* Sea Light. They gave the course line along the Horse Channel, as before.

Thirteen years after the Cheshire Lights had been erected, William Hutchinson, Liverpool's dock master, reported on their success:

> …the losses [to shipping] have been very few, in comparison to what they were before these light-houses were built, which proves their great use to the trade of this place for safety as well as expedition in getting out and in by them.[9]

Liverpool continued to erect lighthouses. In 1781 a new light was installed on Lynas Point. After a gap of fifty years, three more lighthouses were introduced during the 1830s: Black or Perch Rock (New Brighton); Formby and Crosby. Ormeshead was first lit in 1862. Almost all the lighthouses were rebuilt and improved over the years.

The cost of running the lighthouses was recovered from duties paid by ship owners to the dock trust's 'receiver'. The lighthouses were (and most of them still are) strung out along the coast between Anglesey and Formby Point. The chart on p.17 shows their positions and modern names.

## Not Just Lighthouses

In addition to the lighthouses, other guides for mariners were necessary. As early as 1759 a 'floating light for ships going into Hoyle Lake' was fixed onto a buoy. One of the earliest light ships came into being in 1813.

One of the earliest light ships came into being in 1813.

Some fifty years later there were three light vessels and many more buoys. These improvements, together with its excellent pilot service, meant that the port of Liverpool was now among the safest in the country:

> Liverpool has now more foreign trade than London, but from the Mersey the ships go almost direct into the ocean, and wrecks in its neighbourhood are comparatively few [compared with London and the east coast].[10]

By now, the port of Liverpool was respected throughout the maritime world. In November 1852, the dock trust received a request from Lieutenant Thornton A. Jenkins, U.S.N., Secretary of the United States Lighthouse Board. He asked for drawings of the N.W. Lightship, the Bell Beacon and other items 'for use by that Board in organising and improving their system of lights and constructing new light vessels'. The Dock Trust was happy to oblige.

During the latter part of the nineteenth century powerful and manoeuvrable steam-driven vessels were gradually replacing sailing vessels. At the same time, access to the port was steadily improved. Effective dredgers came into use to keep the bar and the channels into the Mersey clear of drifting sand. Later, massive stone revetments were laid against the edges of the sand banks that bordered the channels. By this means, the enormous power of the Mersey's outflow is directed along the channels and sweeps them clear of encroaching sand.[11] By 1913, the route into the river was clearly marked:

> Liverpool Bay and the Mersey and Dee rivers are protected by five light-vessels, named respectively, the *North West, Bar, Formby, Crosby* and the *Dee*, by numerous lights on the piers and points, and by the Bidston and Perch Rock lighthouses. The Perch Rock lies… where the visible shore-line of the river comes to an end, although the course continues to be well marked by buoys and beacons on either side [of the marked channel] for nine miles further down [i.e. as far as the Bar lightship].[12]

## THE OTHER LIGHTHOUSES

Other lighthouses were also built to help mariners when they were in the Mersey estuary. One was opened on the North Wall, near the site of Gladstone Dock, in 1877. It was rebuilt in 1927, when Gladstone Dock was completed. In foggy weather its powerful fog-horn, known as the 'Bootle Bull', bellowed a deep and mournful warning into the gloom that hung over Liverpool Bay. It could be heard, eerily muffled in the swirling mist, along Hoylake promenade, some ten miles distant. When Hoylake upper lighthouse was closed in 1886, two illuminated landmarks were raised at Dove Point, to the east of Hoylake. Another disused lighthouse stands on Hale Point, some miles up-river from Liverpool. It was administered by the Upper Mersey Navigation Commission and operated for 122 years, until it closed in 1958. Just to the north of Woodside Ferry, in Birkenhead,

Hale Point lighthouse.

Point of Ayr Lighthouse.

The original North Wall lighthouse.

Woodside lighthouse.

is a small iron lighthouse, but it is no longer in use either.

Point of Ayr lighthouse, on the west side of the Dee estuary, was originally built and run by the city of Chester. In the early nineteenth century, an abortive effort was made by Liverpool council to take it over. Eventually, however, it came under the jurisdiction of Trinity House.

There have been many changes since the port began with a few perches, buoys and four lighthouses. Now, of the old Liverpool lighthouses, only Point Lynas remains in use. In addition, there is a small lighthouse (more a 'light-mast', in fact) on Hilbre Island. There are no light-ships. Today's ships have immense power and manoeuvrability to hand and they are equipped with radar, radio and satellite navigation systems.

# 1
# Leasowe's Lighthouses
## *The Sea Lights*

*Fires in the night are the sign of mankind's life to an eye at sea.*
Joseph Conrad, *The Unlighted Coast*, 1926.

The early view of Liverpool on p.25 with its forest of masts is especially remarkable because it shows, across the Mersey and the marshy inlet called Wallasey Pool, the *two* Mockbeggar lighthouses at Leasowe. Within a year or so, the lower lighthouse (the one on the right) was to collapse into the sea. The artist seems to have viewed the scene from the vicinity of the Bluecoat School (completed in 1725, now Bluecoat Chambers). St George's church steeple rises from the site of the present-day Queen Victoria memorial, at the end of Castle Street. The tall building on the extreme left of the picture was an early Customs House, at the head of the Old Dock.

### HALF A MILLION GOOD BRICKS

A hundred years after Liverpool opposed Reading's Bill for a lighthouse on the Cheshire shore, great changes had taken place and Liverpool was now a busy port. However, this had brought about a proportionate increase in losses of ships, cargo and lives on the sandbanks of Liverpool Bay. The town's councillors were forced to rethink their policy on lighthouses, and in 1762 parliamentary permission was given to build the four Cheshire Lighthouses. The contract for bricks was put out to tender:

This is to give Notice, by Order of the Committee appointed for carrying on the Building of the Two intended Brick Light-Houses, near Hoy-Lake in the Co. of Chester,

To any Person or Persons, who are willing to contract with them for making of Five Hundred Thousand good Bricks, of the common Size, out of Land lying near to the Place whereon each of such Light Houses is to be erected; the Trespass of getting Clay, and making on such Land, is to be paid for by the Committee. Such Persons are desired to send in their Proposals in Writing, directed to the said Committee at the Mayor's Office, in Liverpool, on or before Monday the Thirty-first Day of January Instant, and attend at Twelve O'Clock at Noon, and give Security for Performance of such Contract.

FRANCIS GILDART, Town-Clerk.[1]

We cannot be certain which two 'Brick Light-Houses' are alluded to here. They were either the two upper lighthouses – the one at Hoylake and the one at Leasowe – or the two lighthouses at Leasowe. There is evidence suggesting that the original plan was for the Sea Lights to be similar to the Lake Lights, i.e., one lighthouse a brick tower and the other a mobile wooden structure.[2] However, this idea was short-lived and it was decided to build two brick towers at Leasowe instead.

The present Leasowe lighthouse is the only original Cheshire Light still standing. Although Hoylake upper and Bidston lighthouses still exist, they are not the original buildings. There is an apocryphal tale that the surviving Leasowe lighthouse, with its 1763 date-stone, was rebuilt in 1824. However, the minutes of the Dock Trust mention only routine maintenance to the lighthouse during 1824, and the rumour has been roundly rebutted, with much supporting evidence, by at least two respected local historians: J.S. Rees[3] and E. Cuthbert Woods[4]. Another historian who agreed with Rees and Woods commented on the construction:

An interesting innovation, due no doubt to the British climate, was the use of cavity-wall construction which was used in the mid-eighteenth century. The 33.5 metre high Leasowe tower on the Mersey which was built in 1763 is a good example. The regular thickness of brick made it possible to separate the outer and inner skin by a uniform cavity.[5]

Unfortunately, no reference is given as to where this particular information originated. William Hutchinson, Liverpool's dock master, would almost certainly have been involved in the design of the building. He stated, in a general discussion about lighthouses, that: 'without there is a small vacuity made in the walls of lighthouses for the wet to drain down, it will beat thro' and rot the wood work'.[6] Surely this is a reference to some kind of cavity wall construction. There is evidence of damp penetration through the walls, but after 250 years the 'small vacuity' may well have been bridged.

*Above:* From *View of the Harbour of Leverpool,* by E. Rooker, 1770. Reproduced with the kind permission of the Liverpool Record Office, Liverpool Libraries.

*Right:* The original Sea Lights

SEA LIGHTS AT MOCKBEGGAR
NEAR HYLE LAKE

## THE EARLY LIGHTS

Once built, the Cheshire Lights were lit by open coal fires in grates. In an attempt to make them burn more steadily they were soon housed in a lantern but, as William Hutchinson explained, there were still serious problems:

> It is well known…that open coal fire light, exposed to all winds and weathers, cannot be made to burn and show a constant steady blaze…for in storms of wind, when lights are most wanted, these open fires are made to burn furiously, and very soon away, so as to melt the very iron work about the grate, and in cold weather, when it snows, hails, or rains hard, the keepers of the lights…are apt to neglect till the fire is too low…and in some weathers it must be difficult to make them burn with any brightness. And when they are inclosed in a glased close-lighthouse, they are apt to smoke the windows greatly…[7]

After a few years of experimentation and trials Hutchinson made what would now be referred to as a 'technological breakthrough' when he devised and introduced a revolutionary new light. This was an oil lamp with a parabolic reflector that concentrated all the light into a single beam. Hutchinson had the new apparatus fitted into the Cheshire Lights around 1770. When Robert Stevenson visited the Mockbeggar lighthouse in 1801, he described the reflector then in use as 'one reflector of silvered glass seven and a half feet diameter and thirteen inches focal distance'.[8]

## A REMOTE AND EERIE SPOT

In the first years of the Mockbeggar lights, the scene on this windswept and isolated part of Cheshire's north coast would have contained the two tall towers, separated by a row of sand hills. At their tops smoky fires blazed through each night. No doubt there would have been a pulley and bucket system to raise the coal for the fires. The shorter Sea Light (80ft high, painted black and white) was sited on the beach, near to the high-water mark; the taller one (101ft high, all-white) was about half a mile to the south-east. The first keepers of the Sea Lights lived and worked at this desolate spot, which was then known as 'The Leasows' or 'Wallasey Leasow'.

Some years later it was discovered that this place was haunted by a long lost past:

> In the surveys [of 1828] which were made by three distinguished engineers…Mr Nimmo discovered a number of human skeletons, nearly opposite the Leasowe Lighthouse, and at the distance of between 100 and 200 yards below the flow of the tide. Their number, and the regularity with which they were deposited, leave no doubt on the mind that this was an ancient place of sepulture; and, owing to the antiseptic qualities of the peaty earth, they may have lain there for many centuries.[9]

About a mile eastwards from the lighthouses stood an octagonal, castellated tower built in 1593 by Ferdinando, the fifth Earl of Derby. Originally called New Hall,

The 'New Hall' and the beginnings of 'Leasowe Castle'[10] (Courtesy of Wallasey Reference Library).

it had been empty for many years and had become known as Mockbeggar Hall; a name that expressed 'the disillusionment of the weary tramp who had gone out of his way to seek food and then found the building deserted'.[11] Thus the new lighthouses were called the 'Mockbeggar' lights. During the early nineteenth century, the New Hall was extended until it was part of a grand house.

In 1802, Margaret Boode, the widow of Lewis William Boode, became its owner. From the time she took it over, it was known as Leasowe Castle, and she made many additions to the hall. She was well respected for generously giving shelter and rest to shipwrecked mariners at a time when others were robbing them.

## THE FIRST KEEPERS

The first keepers of the Leasowe lighthouses were appointed in April 1764. They were John Bennett, in charge of the lower Sea Light, and Alexander Smarley, keeper of the upper Sea Light. An Alexander Smarley was baptised at West Derby in 1745. If, as seems likely, this was the first keeper, he would have been nineteen when he was given this responsible and physically demanding job. With an open fire many hundredweights of coal had to be hauled to the top of the tower. Each night the light-fire had to be stoked into a brightly burning blaze. During the day the keeper would have tended his garden, in which he grew vegetables for himself and fodder for his cow. Any supplies he may have needed would have required a long trek. The job would have been virtually impossible for just one man to carry out; therefore Smarley and Bennet probably helped each other, or maybe they had family help.

By June 1765, Smarley had been replaced by Richard Wilding, whose surname was at times misinterpreted as both Whelden and Welding. He may have been very young (a Richard Wilding was baptised at St George's church, Liverpool, 24 December 1751). In those days, it was normal for young lads of eleven to seek work. When Wilding was married, in 1776, he signed with his mark. The fact that he could not read probably accounts for the phonetic spellings of his name. Richard *Welding* is first referred to in 1765, when he was awarded the huge sum of sixty pounds 'towards the loss he sustained by the accidental burning down of one of the lighthouses in Cheshire'. As to which lighthouse was alluded to here, it is generally accepted that there was a disastrous fire at the upper Sea Light when 'all its inner woodwork was consumed'.[12] Just what caused the fire and why Wilding received such generous compensation (more than three times his annual salary) we may never know.

The Leasowe lighthouses were isolated and exposed, being sited equidistantly between the hamlets of Wallasey and West Kirby and on the edge of the Irish Sea. A year after the lighthouses were built, the keepers received a 25 per cent increase in wages, giving them four pounds a year more than the Hoylake keepers. This was because 'the duty and other inconveniences' at Leasowe 'greatly exceed those at Hoyle Lake'. Two years later, Richard Whelden [*sic*], keeper of the upper Leasowe lighthouse, was rewarded for his good behaviour and compensated for the 'extraordinary duty and fatigue' he endured because of 'the disadvantages of the situation of the Mockbeggar lights from any neighbourhood or supply of provisions'. He was given a huge rise from twenty to twenty-six pounds a year. This was funded, without increasing the overall wage bill, by cutting two pounds from the salaries of each of the other keepers. Thus the Hoylake keepers received £16 pounds each, while Bennet, at the lower Leasowe lighthouse, received £18.

Richard Wilding probably moved to Bidston lighthouse when the new upper Sea Light opened in 1771. Certainly, he was the keeper there in 1779. Unfortunately, no further reference to the keepers of Leasowe lighthouse have been found for the period between 1779 and 1799.

## THE WAYWARD & THE STEADY

Some of the lighthouse keepers appear to have been ready to make extra cash if the opportunity presented itself, perhaps by illicitly turning their lighthouse into an inn or, as in the case of Robert Woods, keeper at Leasowe, helping people who had an unlawful interest in local shipwrecks. On 1 February 1799, Woods was in trouble with his employers because he had 'acted as a wreck looker' on behalf of John Glegg, esquire, who had inherited an ancient right to unclaimed wrecks around parts of the Wirral coast.[13] Woods was brought before the Committee to be reprimanded and warned against future involvement with the unsavoury business of the wreckers. Four years later he appears to have been caught wreck-looking again, but this time he was dismissed. Even as late as 1839, in the *Report of the Royal Commission on the need for a Police Force*, it was stated, with regard to wreckers, that:

Cheshire and Cornwall are the worst. On the Cheshire coast not far from Liverpool, they will rob those who have escaped the perils of the sea and come safe on shore, and mutilate dead bodies for the sake of rings and personal ornaments.[14]

Soon after Woods' dismissal, the Dock Committee made it clear that they were not prepared to accept any more 'irregularities', when they decreed that:

Mr Urmson the Master of Bidston Lighthouse be directed and empowered to visit all the lower lighthouses at least once in every week varying the day and time of his visiting the said houses so that the respective keepers may not know when he may be expected.

The lighthouse appears to have had a period of relative calm during the time of its next keeper, John Smith. There are few incidents recorded and it would seem that Smith simply got on with his job, or perhaps he was just very good at not being caught.

At this time, there were two keepers with the same name: John Smith of Leasowe lighthouse and John Smith of Hoylake lower lighthouse. The latter had taken over from his father, yet another John Smith. Whether the two contemporary John Smiths were related or not hasn't been discovered, but they certainly kept in touch. In January 1810 they jointly petitioned for an increase in pay, which was duly granted. John Smith at lower Hoylake received a 5 guinea (£5.25) increase to 30 guineas, and John Smith at Leasowe was given a similar increase, to 35 guineas.

Conditions at Leasowe, where the land is flat and low-lying, could be particularly bad, especially at high spring tides when the wind was blowing a strong gale off the sea. December 1827 was just such a time:

On Wednesday the 19th, the wind blew from the south-west, a violent gale, which raised the tide from four to five feet above its expected height…The water on that day broke over the Leasowe with resistless fury, inundating the common for several hundred yards inland, and in one part more than half a mile from its ordinary boundary; filling the ditches, pools, and covering the fields and enclosures of the poor cottagers, sweeping away many of their fences, saturating their gardens, pastures, and tillage land with salt water, thereby rendering them comparatively barren for several years to come, even if they should be preserved free from another similar visitation. The Leasowe lighthouse was encompassed with water, flowing up to the kitchen steps, and beating the ground with such violence as to leave large hollows within a few yards of the building.[15]

For John Smith, life must have become harder with the destruction of his plot and the contamination of the well. He struggled on for another three years, and then, on 10 August 1830, he retired, his employers noting that he had 'from age, become incapable of properly executing the duties of that office'. He was given a pension of ten shillings per week, and never had to make the weary climb to the top of Leasowe lighthouse again.

## THE LONGEST TENURE

John Jones and his wife Ann, a young married couple from Denbigh, came to live at the lighthouse in 1830, when he was twenty-six and she was twenty-seven. Since the erection of the lighthouse, almost seventy years before, changes had gradually taken place. The area was no longer as lonely and isolated. One or two cottages had been built nearby, for embankment workers and there were other, more substantial dwellings, such as Bankfield House, which was erected in 1790. Following the recent death of Mrs Boode, Leasowe Castle had become a hotel.

The first years at the lighthouse for the Jones's, appear to have been uneventful until the Great Storm, which caused widespread devastation in January 1839. Many lives were lost both locally and nationally, and there was considerable damage to property. Across the Wirral and especially near the coast, numerous buildings were destroyed. Just three miles away, at Wallasey, the parish church was:

> …almost wholly unroofed, and the outbuildings of the hall below, belonging to Sir John Tobin, are stripped. In the village the destruction has been considerable, particularly in thatched buildings. All the farmsteads on the North Shore of the Wirral peninsula have suffered more or less. Hay-stacks, etc. have been blown away.[16]

The sandbanks of Liverpool Bay were strewn with numerous wrecks. John Jones gave evidence at the subsequent enquiry, which was held at Leasowe Castle. He stated that he had sighted a body floating near the water's edge and, having recovered it, found that it showed slight signs of life. It was William Douglas, a passenger from the American packet ship *Pennsylvania*.[17] She had run aground heavily and broken up, about three miles off-shore. Jones told the enquiry that, with assistance, he immediately carried Mr Douglas to Leasowe Castle where:

> …every possible exertion was made to restore animation, by stripping him, placing him before a large fire in a blanket, and rubbing him with hot salt in flannel; but without any appearance of returning vitality.[18]

The grave of William Douglas is in Wallasey parish churchyard beside that of the mate of the *Pennsylvania*, Lucus Blydenburgh. Although the storm lasted only a few days, bodies of the victims continued to be washed onto the local beaches for the rest of that year. At Wallasey, apart from Douglas and Blydenburgh, eleven more bodies were found. Further along the coast, at Hoylake, five unidentified men and a female child were washed up and buried in the new Holy Trinity churchyard.

Every bad storm along the Wirral coast brought its toll of fine sailing vessels wrecked on the sandbanks and inevitable loss of life. Consequently, Hoylake's parish records show that during the ten years from 1836 to 1845, thirty-four of the sixty-one people buried there had been washed up on the beach.[19]

Since Mrs Boode's time, Leasowe Castle had been used, in the aftermath of severe storms, as a hospital, mortuary and coroner's office. After the Great Storm, it became the centre of public and press interest:

> The fine Hotel, known as Leasowe Castle…has, since the hurricane, been the scene of great and melancholy interest. The situation of the hotel…has long rendered it a place of refuge to the survivors from shipwrecks…From Tuesday…up to yesterday, an unusual number of persons in vehicles, on horseback, and on foot, continued to pass from the several ferries on the Mersey to the Castle, many actuated by curiosity, and several (relatives of parties in the wrecked vessels) to learn the worst.[20]

Curtailing the activities of the curious and the criminal was a priority. Wallasey had no police force of its own, so help from outside had to be sought:

> The Liverpool police were early on the alert, not only on the Lancashire shore, adjacent to the town, but on the Cheshire coast. No fewer than thirty constables were stationed along the Leasowe shore for the rescue or preservation of life and property, besides twelve who were placed as near as possible on board of the stranded ships. The exertions of Mr Whitty, Mr Dowling and indeed of all connected with the police establishment have been above arduous, praiseworthy, and highly efficient.[21]

The main reason for the unusually heavy police presence at the scene of the disaster was the tradition of 'wrecking' among the locals. This term was once applied to those who lured ships onto the shore with spurious lights. However, by the early 1800s, 'wreckers' meant anyone who plundered property that came ashore from wrecked ships, including stealing from the bodies of victims.

Inevitably, the lighthouse keepers were often helpless witnesses of the disasters in Liverpool Bay. However, the routine of watch-keeping and tending the light was the main part of their job. In 1840 the salaries at Hoylake and Leasowe lighthouses were reviewed in the light of the keepers' workloads. At the time, upper Hoylake's keeper received more than Leasowe's. Following the review the Hoylake salaries were equalised at £45 because they each had two reflectors to maintain. Leasowe's keeper, however, had his salary increased by 50 per cent, to £60 because he had eight reflectors to look after and there were 140 steps up the old wooden stairs to the lantern.

At last then, John Jones was properly compensated for the hardships he had to endure. And yet, just over a year later, his employers received a complaint that he had been absent from work for over a week, leaving his wife and the servant girl to carry out his duties. His dismissal was considered, but, instead he was called before the Committee, reprimanded for breach of duty, and cautioned.

Mr Jones worked steadily for the next few years. However, following a severe accident in 1849, his wife asked for some 'pecuniary assistance' because of the heavy expenses that had ensued. Usually a few pounds would be granted from the Charitable Fund, but in this instance Ann Jones's application was declined. A harsh decision, but perhaps the accident was not work-related.

Leasowe lighthouse in 1840.

A year later the region was assailed by yet another severe storm which caused several shipwrecks on the sand banks, including that of the *Providence*, where a dramatic rescue took place:

> She was met by the pilot-boat, and conducted to the Horse Channel. Here William Parry, of No. 4 pilot-boat, volunteered his services, and jumped from the pilot-boat, to the ship, although the sea was running mountains high. This vessel being in a disabled state, he endeavoured to bring her up with her anchors off the bight of Hoyle, but she drifted and went on shore. The pilot and a number of the crew found their way over the bank and were saved.[22]

For John Jones and his family this storm brought more trouble. Over the years the land around the lighthouse had been turned into a smallholding. Here they kept a cow and grew vegetables – an essential part of their existence. All his hard work was swept away during the few hours of the storm:

> ...when the land around the lighthouse was overflowed by the sea, which caused the destruction of the whole of the crop of potatoes, turnips and winter fodder for his cow.

Jones appealed to his employers for help and was allowed the sum of £10 'to relieve him from the loss he has sustained during the great gale'.

## THE EMBANKMENT

Ninety years earlier, when the lighthouse was built, the land was protected by a high ridge of sand hills and mill grass. Over time this natural barrier had eroded leaving no defence against the encroachment of the sea. Even though an embankment had been under construction since 1829 it was still far from adequate. In 1851 Liverpool's Marine Surveyor reported the difficulty of access to the lighthouse due to the constant flooding of the approach road. This report was sent to the Commission for the Embankment of Leasowe. However, almost two years later nothing had been done, so the Marine Surveyor submitted another report asserting that it was 'highly necessary that a road should be made to the Leasowe lighthouse, the passage of coals, oil and other stores being impracticable'.

Another four years elapsed and the embankment problem had still not been properly addressed. In 1855, expressing concern about the problems affecting the land around the lighthouse, a spot which was regularly flooded, the Marine Surveyor, William Lord, was apprehensive about the wider consequences. Again he wrote to the Commissioners:

> The sea embankment at Leasowe has again sustained serious injury, from the high tides and heavy gales of the present winter, its total destruction at one period, being imminent. The sea has for many years past, been encroaching on the sand hills in the vicinity, and, should a disruption, and demolition of the Leasowe embankment, take place at high water of a spring tide during a gale from the north west, the consequences would be most disastrous to the navigation of the Mersey.

Although more work was done to strengthen the structure, it was to be almost a century before a fully effective embankment was built, long after the lighthouse had been closed down.

## MRS JONES TAKES OVER

The hard conditions at Leasowe lighthouse seem to have been too much for John Jones. In 1853 Sir Edward Cust, the incumbent of Leasowe Castle (still used as a hotel[23]), reported Jones's drunkenness to his employers. On receipt of a note from Jones expressing 'great contrition', the Dock Trust severely reprimanded him. However, the following year Jones was again reported, this time 'for intoxication and insubordination'. He was dismissed and his wife appointed in his place, on a salary of £60, on condition that she employ a competent assistant. If she hadn't replaced her husband, the couple would have lost their home as well as their income. Ann Jones thus became the first woman keeper of Leasowe lighthouse, with Ellen Jones, her young servant. Although the Dock Committee often seemed very parsimonious, they generally behaved well towards women in their employ and, surprisingly, women usually received equal pay for the same work long before equal pay became common practice in other fields. After Jones was dismissed he continued to live in the lighthouse until his death in 1857. A different side to John Jones' character is revealed on his gravestone, on which is inscribed: 'his bereaved widow and affectionate friends sorrow deep' and records that he 'suffered much yet patience had he'.[24]

Life for Ann Jones and her young assistant must have been gruelling. Even comparatively simple jobs, such as heating and cooking, required a great deal of effort. Every year twelve tons of coal were delivered free to the lighthouse for domestic use. This amounts to about four and a half bags of coal each week, throughout the year. Each bag would have weighed about 50kg. If the fire was to burn efficiently buckets of coal had to be hauled up to the kitchen range every day and large amounts of cinders and ash cleared out regularly. Mrs Jones probably kept the kitchen range going continuously and, as the tower tends to be quite cold even in summer, the fire in the sitting room may well have been lit all the year round. Fortunately, the wash house range was on the ground floor near to where the coal was stored. By 1857 it was worn out and a new cottage range was purchased from William O'Dell, a local merchant, which cost about 25s. (£1.25). Mrs Jones' main task, of course, was to keep the light burning throughout the night, and this too was hard physical work, up and down to the lantern each night, trimming the wick, topping up the oil and checking that the light was burning brightly. As well as her other chores the smallholding had to be tended and the animals fed and looked after.

Mrs Jones and her young assistant struggled with the arduous conditions and tasks at Leasowe lighthouse for another six years until Ann Jones died on 23 July 1867, aged sixty-five. She was buried with her husband in Hoylake churchyard. Ann Jones had lived and worked at the lighthouse for thirty-seven years, including nearly thirteen years as its keeper.


## THE MORGANS

For just over a hundred years, as far as we know, there had been no children living at Leasowe lighthouse. All that changed when Joseph Morgan, a Scotsman from Fort William, became keeper. He set up home with his wife Jane, (from Whitehaven) and their five children; two boys and three girls. Three years later, in 1870, Mrs Morgan had another child, whom they named Graham. Graham Morgan may have been the first child to be born in the lighthouse.

Soon after he arrived at the lighthouse Morgan applied to his employers to allow him a pony and cart 'for the purpose of conveying stores and water to the lighthouse', but his application was denied. Apparently though, the keepers were able to borrow a horse from a local farmer, which would have made things easier.

The Morgans turned the lighthouse into a family home and so it remained for the rest of its working time. The interior layout of the lighthouse (shown below) was as follows: on the ground floor, the large space was used for storage; the first floor was the kitchen with the range; above this was the living room with an open coal fire; the next three floors were available as bedrooms and there was a small, windowless storeroom above. At the top was the lantern. There was, therefore, plenty of room for the Morgan family.

By 1880, Morgan's health had deteriorated and he was unable to cope with the onerous job of looking after the tall lighthouse. His employers decided to exchange him with the keeper of Hoylake's upper lighthouse, where the accommodation is on two floors and there are far fewer steps to climb to the lantern.

## THE BELLS

Thomas Ward Bell had previously been the keeper at both the lower and upper Hoylake lighthouses before moving to Leasowe. Originally from Bangor, Northern Ireland, he brought his extended family with him; his wife Elizabeth Ann (Liverpool-born), and their four children ranging in age from three years to nineteen.

The Bells were well-used to the lighthouse way of life with three of their children having been born at Hoylake. They were also able to accommodate Mrs Bell's mother, Elizabeth Evans, who acted as housekeeper to the family and Mrs Bell's invalid sister. Ten years later the eldest daughter had left home, but the Bells had their four year-old grandson Joshua staying with them. There were also two visitors – Ernest Brown, a London perfume manufacturer and William E. Brocklebank, a solicitor's clerk. With so many people staying at the lighthouse it must have been a tight squeeze, especially considering that they were not all family members.

Mr Bell was well past retiring age when he died aged seventy-one in 1892. At the age of sixty, Mrs Bell was either unwilling to take over from her husband, or the Dock Board considered her unsuitable. For the Bell family, life must suddenly have become very difficult. The household consisted of Mrs Bell, her two unmarried and unemployed daughters, and her fifteen year-old plumber's apprentice son. Her disabled sister-in-law and possibly her five-year-old grandson also lived there. Mrs Bell had lost not only her husband, the main breadwinner, but also her home. She was not offered a pension. Instead, she received a single payment of £25, the equivalent of four month's wages. Without the security of the Welfare State, especially after the loss of the breadwinner, many families faced hardship and uncertainty in Victorian times. Soon a new family occupied Leasowe lighthouse, and the Bells were left to fend for themselves.

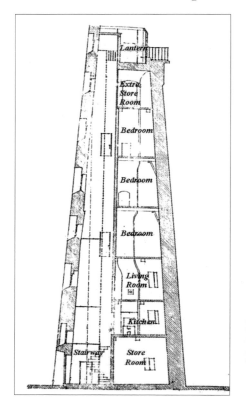

*Above left:* Sectional view of Leasowe lighthouse.

*Above right:* Leasowe lighthouse *c.*1900.

## THE LAST KEEPERS

When Thomas Williams was transferred from Hoylake upper to Leasowe lighthouse, he brought with him his wife and nine of their children. Once more the lighthouse was a family home, with five girls and four boys ranging in age from one to twenty-two years of age. Mrs Williams later had one more child, a girl, shortly after arriving at Leasowe. In all, she had had thirteen children, two of whom died in infancy.

The portraits of Mr and Mrs Williams were painted by Frank T. Copnall. A local artist, he turned professional in 1897 at the age of twenty-seven and became well-known as a painter of Liverpool dignitaries.[25] Given that Mr Williams died in 1894, this picture must have been painted when Copnall was an amateur in his early twenties.

This is one of the few pictures we have of a Liverpool lighthouse keeper in his official uniform, holding the standard-issue telescope. Uniform for the keepers had been introduced in 1864. At first it consisted of a frock coat and a silk or felt hat, but around the time of the Williams's move to Leasowe the uniform was changed to a reefer jacket with a peaked cap.

When his picture was painted, Mr Williams appears to have been in good health. Unfortunately, by May 1894 his health had seriously deteriorated and he wrote out his will, leaving almost everything he owned to his wife. He left what must have been some of his most prized possessions; 'all my joiners and other tools', to his son, Job, assistant telegraph keeper at South Stack. A few months later Mr Williams died, leaving Mrs Williams with at least eight children to care for, including the baby who was only one year-old.

Unlike Mrs Bell, Mrs Williams was able to take over as keeper, with the help of her children, including Job, her eldest son, who later resigned his position as second keeper at Ormeshead lighthouse and came back to Leasowe. Officially Mrs Williams didn't have an assistant, but the Williams family seem to have been very close and would, undoubtedly, have helped their mother.

Many changes took place at the lighthouse at the beginning of 1898. These were precipitated by the disastrous Crosby lighthouse fire that caused the death of the keeper, his wife and a visitor. Leasowe, potentially, was even more vulnerable than Crosby because of the way the lighthouse was used. At Leasowe the family lived and worked in the tower, whereas all the other land-based lights operated by Liverpool, (Lynas, the upper and lower Hoylake lights, Crosby and Bidston) had been rebuilt, with the keepers living in cottages alongside the lighthouse.

At the inquest into the deaths at Crosby, certain specific recommendations were made if the lighthouse was to be rebuilt:

[The lighthouse] should be built in accordance with all the latest improvements and safeguards [e.g., replacement of the wooden staircase with an iron or stone one] and an assistant keeper should be provided.

*Above left:* Thomas Williams, in uniform with his telescope.

*Above right:* Mary Elizabeth Williams, Leasowe's last keeper.

In the event, Crosby wasn't rebuilt, but the Dock Board suddenly became aware of the dangers and was quick to act upon the recommendations in relation to Leasowe. After some discussion it was decided:

> to arrange for an iron staircase with iron sheeting on the doors leading from the staircase, to be substituted for the present wooden staircase at the said Lighthouse, at an estimated cost of £250, and also for the provision of a new Oil Store and Tanks and for the carrying out of the work suggested by him [the Coroner] in the Light Room and at the lower portion of the Tower to protect it from possible danger from fire in the out buildings at an estimated cost of £150.

The meeting was held in private, which meant that there were no reporters present. This suggests the Board was afraid that damaging criticism may be levelled at them in the aftermath of the Crosby fire.

The provision of an assistant keeper was relatively easy and cheap to implement at Leasowe. Thus Mrs Williams' eldest daughter, twenty-five-year-old Rose, was appointed to the position at twelve shillings per week, providing there was nothing in the various Acts to prevent a woman taking on the job. Considering that Mrs Jones had been appointed lighthouse keeper more than forty years earlier it seems a little late to wonder whether or not it was legal to employ women. The conditions attached to the appointment also stipulated that Rose would not be eligible for any allowance, pension or monetary payment beyond the basic wage. Other young women had been assistant keepers in the past, for instance, Mrs Jones's servant girl. None had so much red tape attached as this appointment, with a special memo detailing Rose Williams' duties:

1. She is to assist in the work at the lighthouse, including the watching of the lamps, whilst they are burning.
2. She is to act under the directions and orders of the keeper.
3. The accommodation to be used by her, in the lighthouse, to be subject to the direction of the keeper.
4. No allowance for coals will be made to her.

One of the main problems at the Crosby fire had been the poor water supply which had considerably hampered the efforts of the fire brigade. Therefore, within a couple of months of the fire, another important safety feature was incorporated at Leasowe, the installation of a fire hydrant. As there was no mains water, negotiations were initiated with the Hoylake & West Kirby Gas and Water Co. Ltd. A 3in water main had to be run about half a mile, from Station Road (now called Pasture Road) to the lighthouse gates. However, there is no mention of giving the residents of the lighthouse the convenience of a running water supply.

*Above:* The lighthouse, with attached outhouses, etc., 1936. Reproduced with the kind permission of the *Liverpool Daily Post*.

*Right:* Leasowe lighthouse *c.*2000.

## The Final Years

The new century saw Mrs Williams continuing as keeper with the help of her large family. Rose Williams resigned her position in October 1900 and was replaced by her seventeen-year-old sister Bertha, who was paid ten shillings per week and life henceforth continued pretty much as usual. However, changes had already begun to take place with the closure of upper Hoylake lighthouse in 1886. With improved aids to navigation in the approach to Liverpool, the usefulness of the Cheshire lights was almost over.

In March 1908, a memo from the Marine Surveyor suggested that the lighthouses needed painting even though they 'may shortly be discontinued, the buildings will still remain as useful survey marks'. However, within four months both lighthouses had closed. Mrs Williams was retained as the caretaker with a wage of £1 per week, but she was also given the customary coal issue and was allowed to live rent and rates free. The announcement of the closures of the two lighthouses, on July 15 1908, was printed in the local newspapers. After 145 years the lights were finally dimmed at Leasowe.

Mrs Williams' retirement prospects were rather better than those of Mrs Bell. In August 1909, the Dock Board recommended that Mrs Williams, now acting as caretaker of the lighthouse, should be:

> permitted to retire from the Board's service and that a superannuation allowance after the rate of 15/- [75p] per week be granted to her, during the pleasure of the Board, as from the 2nd September, inclusive, also that the Premises in question be advertised to be let.

Seventeen years after arriving at Leasowe lighthouse, in November 1909, Mrs Williams left. The Williams family stayed in the area and each summer ran a teashop, available to the many hundreds of visitors who camped on Leasowe Common. She died in 1935 and was buried with her husband and two of her children in Hoylake's Holy Trinity churchyard.

John Austin, keeper of the telegraph station at Liverpool, moved into the lighthouse when Mrs Williams moved out. He was permitted to reside there free of rent, rates and taxes and lived there until the end of 1920. In 1930 the lighthouse was finally sold to the County Borough of Wallasey for £900.

For many years the lighthouse was left to the vandals and decay. Then, in 1989, *The Friends of Leasowe Lighthouse* was formed. The restoration began: windows were replaced, a replica iron staircase was installed and, where necessary, floors were repaired. Plans have been drawn up to reinstate the outbuildings to accommodate a purpose-built exhibition centre and Rangers' office. The lighthouse is a popular and valuable resource for local schools and the community. It is open to the public on a regular basis.

# 2
# Bidston Lighthouse
## The New Sea Light & Signal Station

*Oh! Dream of joy! Is this indeed*
*The lighthouse top I see?*
*Is this the hill? Is this the kirk?*
*Is this mine own countree?*

Samuel Taylor Coleridge, *The Ancient Mariner*, 1798

### AN ELEVATED LIGHTHOUSE

When the original lower Sea Light at Leasowe collapsed into the sea in 1770 there was much debate about the siting of the new light. Coastal erosion was a major problem, and the authorities didn't want to run the risk of the new lighthouse being undermined by the sea. A novel solution was eventually reached. The lighthouse would be built two miles inland on Bidston Hill. Negotiations with the owner of the land, Mr Vyner, were successful. The following year, permission having been obtained by an Act of Parliament, the replacement lighthouse was built on a sandstone ridge with a commanding view over Liverpool Bay and the River Mersey.

Hilton's picture (see p.43) depicts a very different aspect, even in 1880, from the one we see today. The view now is of a complex motorway junction, railway lines and, just below the Breck, streets of houses. Then, there was a clear view across Bidston Moss and plain, to Bidston Hill with, from the left, the windmill, observatory and lighthouse.

Bidston lighthouse was quite different from Leasowe as it was an octagonal, four-storey tower made from the local stone rather than brick. It was 244ft above half-tide level and half the height of Leasowe. As with the other Cheshire Lights it was a beacon, with one fixed white light. The disposition of the new Sea Lights is illustrated on Burdett's chart below.

This new lighthouse then, became the upper Sea Light, its alignment with the remaining Leasowe lighthouse giving the course bearing along the Horse Channel, as did the original Sea Lights.

## BIDSTON'S FIRST KEEPER

Richard Wilding was probably the first keeper. He had previously been at Leasowe, but no record has been found of his actual relocation. What is known is that he married Elizabeth McCabe, of the parish of Liverpool, on 4 July 1776, the original American Independence Day. Relations with America were still strained and were not improved by a worrying incident in 1779:

> In this year considerable alarm was excited in Liverpool by the appearance, in the Irish Sea, of some vessels of war of the enemy, under the command of the noted and daring adventurer, Paul Jones, and by his having attacked Whitehaven, and set fire to the shipping there.[1]

Whitehaven is some eighty miles up the coast from Liverpool, so a 'Special Council' was convened to consider how the port should be protected. Various measures were decided upon to improve security; the pilots were instructed to keep watch off Point Lynas and specific instructions were issued to Bidston's keeper ordering that:

> Richard Wilding; upon any Intelligence of an Enemy give an alarm at Bidston Lighthouse, and not keep the Lights burning either there or at Hoylake in such case.

Fortunately Paul Jones' incursion at Whitehaven was not repeated, so the lights were kept burning along the Cheshire coast.

As well as his lighthouse duties, Richard Wilding was also responsible for the signal station on Bidston Hill. This had been in existence for some years before the lighthouse was built. A series of flags and boards was used to relay information about the approach and movement of shipping in Liverpool Bay to the merchants of Liverpool. In 1790 Richard Welding (*sic*) complained that: 'his distinguishing Boards and Public signal flags are much decayed and worn out'.

These signals were an important part of the port's operations, providing a speedy way of transmitting information before the invention of the electric telegraph. When a ship arrived in port, all the facilities for docking and unloading would be ready, thus saving the ship owner time and money. It is no surprise then that the new boards and signals were immediately refurbished under the direction of Mr Hutchinson. During the early part of the nineteenth century the flag system was extended until, by 1826, it covered the full length of the ridge. The scene was captured in the writings of a Victorian artist and writer:

*Above: The View of Bidston Hill from Wallasey Breck* by Henry Hilton, 1880. Bidston windmill, observatory and lighthouse can be seen on top of Bidston Hill, top left. (Reproduced with the kind permission of the Williamson Art Gallery and Museum, Birkenhead; Wirral Museums Service).

*Right:* Leasowe lighthouse with the original Bidston lighthouse, seen above and behind it.

*Below:* The signal flags erected along the ridge of Bidston Hill.

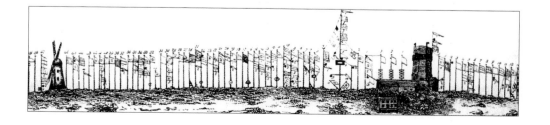

They passed under the walls of the lighthouse, with its array of signal masts that looked as if somebody was either preparing a great display of fireworks, or making ready to set sail, and carry the entire hill, lighthouse , telegraph, and all, out to sea, upon the first fair wind.[2]

## WILLIAM HUTCHINSON, DOCK MASTER

William Hutchinson became a pivotal figure in the development of the Port of Liverpool. A native of Newcastle-upon-Tyne he had worked his way up from cabin boy to master and part owner of the privateer, *Liverpool*.[3] His exploits with Captain Fortunatus Wright, another well known privateer, were legendary. Undoubtedly the worst moment of Hutchinson's sea career was the occasion when the vessel he was on ran out of food and water. Lots were drawn among the starving men as to who should be killed and eaten. Hutchinson lost. Providentially, another ship hove into view and he was spared. For the rest of his life Hutchinson observed the day of his deliverance as a special day of thanksgiving.

In 1759 he was appointed Liverpool's Dock Master and worked unceasingly for the good of the port and for seafarers. Over a period of twenty-five years he kept a series of observations of the tides, barometer, weather and winds, the first five years of which became the basis for Holden's Tide Tables.[4] However, his industry and commitment to the safety of mariners was paramount, and he was instrumental in bringing about a revolutionary improvement to the lighting apparatus used in lighthouses. The inspiration for his new invention is reputed to have come from a wager in a coffee house. One of the men present wagered that he could read a newspaper from a distance of 30ft, in a darkened room, by the light of a farthing candle. The trick was to concentrate all of the feeble light into one direction. He did this by lining the inside of a bowl with putty and pressing into it a mirror glass mosaic. The wager was won. Hutchinson, who had been present at the meeting, was intrigued by the idea and felt it could be used to great advantage in the Cheshire Lights. His experiments resulted in a parabolic reflector that focused all the light of a naked flame into a single, powerful beam. The new reflector was first used at Bidston lighthouse.[5] It is such an important part of lighthouse history that a replica of the reflector is on display at Trinity House headquarters in London.

Not content with his full time job as Dock Master, Mr Hutchinson also managed to find time to write a number of books on seamanship. One, *A Treatise on Practical Seamanship*, earned him a ten-guinea award from Liverpool Corporation, 'it being deemed a book of great utility to commercial places'. In order to keep up with any new developments in lighthouse design Hutchinson travelled to the east coast in 1781 to 'inspect several lighthouses there'.

As well as overseeing the building of the Cheshire lighthouses he was also a prime mover in many other key improvements at the port of Liverpool, including the establishment of the lifeboat and pilot services and the Liverpool Marine Society, 'founded in 1789 for the benefit of masters of vessels, widows and children'[6].

Replica of William Hutchinson's
parabolic reflector, displayed at
Trinity House.

William Hutchinson, Dock
Master 1759–1793.

William Hutchinson's commitment to Liverpool was unwavering. He finally retired in 1793 and died in 1801 aged eighty-five.[7] A contemporary said of him: 'his whole life was one unwearied scene of industrious usefulness'.[8]

## LIVERPOOL'S FIRST WOMAN KEEPER

The Dock Committee's minutes tend to concentrate on the day-to-day running of the lighthouses, so there are many entries concerned with their upkeep and such things as the buying of lamp oil. The keepers were usually only mentioned when they were appointed, got into trouble, or died, but occasionally we get a glimpse into their way of life:

In April 1797, when Richard Wilding died, the Dock Committee considered the pay and conditions for his successor. They decided on an annual salary totalling £50, which included an allowance of £20 for the signal work and £4 for coal. The addition to this resolution reveals how the Wildings had run the lighthouse premises up to that point:

> The Committee do also further Report they are of Opinion that the Order forbidding this Lighthouse any longer to continue a Licensed Alehouse will be the means of remedying the Irregularity and Objections formerly made on that account...

Richard Wilding's widow, Elizabeth, was chosen to replace him and was the first female keeper appointed by Liverpool. Chester trustees were, in fact, ahead of Liverpool when they appointed Mrs Cormes as keeper at Point of Ayr's lighthouse in 1791. On Elizabeth Wilding's appointment carefully worded conditions of employment were set out:

> Elizabeth Wilding Widow of the late Richard Wilding . . . is hereby appointed Keeper of the Bidston Lighthouse in Cheshire at the clear annual Salary of Fifty Pounds so long as she shall continue to behave herself properly and attentively and employ her Son in Law Captain William Urmson as her Assistant and shall not attempt to employ or use the said Building called the Bidston Lighthouse or any of its Appendages as a Publick House.

To appreciate the Dock Committee's concerns one has to understand the situation of the lighthouse and its proximity to the village. Bidston is not mentioned in Domesday but for many centuries it was the archetypal English village, tucked away at the bottom of Bidston Hill. By 1665, when the pictorial map below was drawn, most of the elements which constituted the village were in place; the church, Bidston Hall and the farmhouses. Thus the Wildings would have joined a settled community where things had remained unchanged for centuries.

A dominant feature of the parish was the flat plain of Moreton lying to the north of the village. The 'towne mosse', usually known today as Bidston Moss, was difficult and dangerous terrain before it was drained.

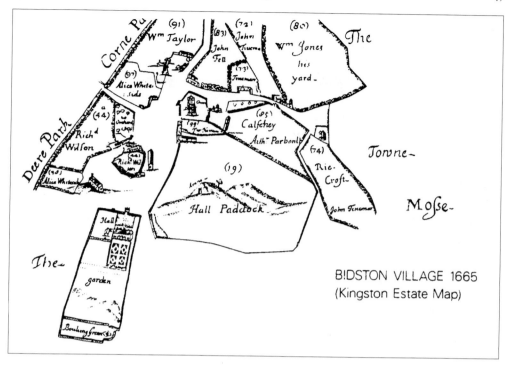

Bidston Village in 1665 (Kingston Estate Map). Reproduced with the kind permission of the Merseyside Archaeological Society.

Bidston Hall, painted by Edward Goodall in 1816. The Lighthouse is on the extreme right. (Reproduced with the permission of Williamson Art Gallery and Museum, Birkenhead; Wirral Museums Service)

Nevertheless, legend has it that smugglers carried their contraband from the coast and 'many a laden pack-horse was led under cover of darkness, across the boggy Bidston Moss',[9] to the *Ring O'Bells* inn.

By 1801 there were 199 people living in the parish of Bidston. However, the parish at that time covered a wider area than it does today. It consisted of the townships of Moreton, Claughton, Saughall Massie and Bidston, so the population was spread out and not just contained within the village itself. In the village the church and the old hall were the main buildings.

Many of the old farmhouses and cottages remain to this day, including Stone Farm which, in the Wildings' time, was the village inn then called the *Ring O'Bells*. It seems the Wildings had decided that they could provide an alternative venue to the inn and were using the lighthouse as a 'licensed alehouse' for any passing trade. A contemporary account confirms that this was indeed the case:

> It is very usual, in summer and fine weather, for parties to cross the river and walk to the [Bidston] lighthouse. The road is good, and the walk, if a trouble, is amply repaid by the charming and extensive prospect which is there displayed. Ale, and bread and cheese, is the only fare to be met with there; except perhaps a cup of tea. Any kind of provision that may be carried thither, will be comfortably dressed and served, and every deficiency compensated by the civility of the occupiers. To those who have not examined a lighthouse, it will, of course, prove a curiosity.[10]

After Mrs Wilding and Captain Urmson took over, the prohibition on alcohol seems to have been adhered to, because there is no further mention of illicit drinking at Bidston lighthouse. However, the concern that lighthouses should not be used by drinkers appears regularly in Council resolutions and the evidence shows that, over the years, drinking was the cause of trouble in some of the other lighthouses.

A feature of the majority of lighthouses in the Liverpool Bay area is the reliance placed on family help; all but one of the lights being land-based. Working conditions on a land-based lighthouse are quite different from those on a rock lighthouse, where the keeper's sole function is to tend the light. In a land-based lighthouse there may well be extra duties such as 'signals work' or looking after the lifeboat station. Added to that the keeper usually needed some sort of garden, and perhaps a shed for a cow to provide food and milk for the family. Mrs Wilding, having been a keeper's wife for over twenty years, would have had a great deal of experience.

However, there were certain underlying problems. Just two years later, in October 1799, tensions between Mrs Wilding and her son-in-law, Captain Urmson, seem to have come to a head, as it was stated that they were not behaving 'properly and attentively'. The report continued:

> Disputes have arisen between Elizabeth Wilding keeper of the Bidston Lighthouse and William Urmson her assistant whereby the Regular Discharge of the very important duties of that appointment may be much endangered.

The disputes referred to coincided with the death of Mrs Wilding's daughter, Mary, who was married to William Urmson. This meant that as well as running the lighthouse, Mrs Wilding probably had to look after her four grandchildren and possibly her son-in-law as well. No wonder 'disputes' had arisen. Whatever the reason for the trouble the Dock Committee was not sympathetic and threatened that 'measures' would be taken to replace either Mrs Wilding or Captain Urmson, or both of them, if things weren't sorted out. Perhaps things settled down, but anyway, less than a year later, the situation was resolved by the death of Mrs Wilding. Her son-in-law Captain Urmson then became the next keeper.

Mrs Wilding's will reveals that she was quite a wealthy woman. Apart from leaving £20 to William Urmson, £20 each to her nephews and nieces and £20 each to her executors, she also left £5 to be distributed amongst 'Poor Persons in the Township of Bidston'.

Having sorted out the smaller bequests, Mrs Wilding (nee McCabe) then dealt with the rest of her estate. Although it is not stated in the parish records, Elizabeth McCabe appears to have been a widow with two daughters when she married Richard Wilding. Her daughter, Mary, married Captain William Urmson in 1787 and had four children, but Mary died the year before her mother. Mrs Wilding's property – two houses in Liverpool – was sold and the money put in trust, 'towards the maintenance and education and bringing up of the children of my late daughter Mary Urmson,' until they were twenty-one. Mrs Wilding's other daughter was also married with children. Oddly Elizabeth Wilding does not name this second daughter, but what she does say is revealing:

> And I give to my daughter the use of my Furniture and Cloaths (sic) for her separate use during her life free from the power of her Husband…

It would appear that Mrs Wilding didn't think much of this son-in-law, nor did she leave him a bequest of £20 as she had to William Urmson. The executors of her will invested in a bond with Liverpool town council which was redeemed in 1817, in accordance with her wishes, when the children had attained their majority. The value of the bond was then £520, quite a sizeable sum in those days (about ten year's salary for a lighthouse keeper).

## A New Broom

Two years after taking over as keeper of Bidston lighthouse, William Urmson remarried. His new wife took on the care of his four children. At about the same time Bidston was visited by Robert Stevenson, who had learned about lighthouse building from his stepfather Thomas Smith. By 1801 Stevenson had built a number of lighthouses in Scotland and, to extend his knowledge further, he decided to make a tour of English lighthouses. This tour 'would, he hoped, teach him about the conditions of the English coast and make an interesting comparison to his work in Scotland'.[11] Stevenson cast a professional eye over the Cheshire lighthouses and described Bidston light in detail as being lit by oil:

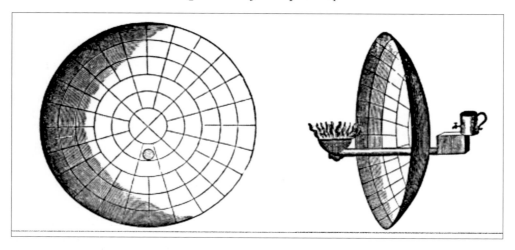

Parabolic Reflector used in the Cheshire Lighthouses, the reflector was formed from wood and lined with pieces of mirror-glass or of plates of tin. The oil was kept on a level with the flame by a dripping-pot that supplied the reservoir behind the reflector.[12]

with one reflector of silvered glass, which is no less than thirteen and a half feet diameter and its focus four feet. This immense reflector is illuminated by one large cotton wick which consumes one gallon of oil in four hours.[13]

However, Stevenson had reservations about some aspects of the design:

I cannot see any good reason for expending such a quantity of oil for one reflector as the same quantity would answer for thirty reflectors of twenty inches diameter, and I am confident that seven such reflectors would give an equal if not superior light.

He did, however, concede that 'this lighthouse is remarkably well taken care of being in every respect clean and in good order'.[14] This is a great tribute to William Urmson, as none of the other Cheshire Lights received this compliment and Stevenson was not given to handing out praise freely. It's especially noteworthy as Urmson, at that time, was a single parent.

In addition to his own lighthouse and the signals, Urmson's workload was increased further by yet another decree from the Dock Committee. He was directed to visit the lighthouses at Leasowe and Hoylake at least once a week. Not only that, but he was instructed to vary the day and time he went, so that the keepers wouldn't know when he was coming, and to report any irregularities or disorderly conduct. Effectively, he was to act as a spy for the Dock Trust. The keepers at the other lighthouses were warned that Captain Urmson was to be regarded as their Superior Officer. This order followed the recent dismissal of Leasowe's keeper, who may have been acting as a 'wreck looker'.

Sometimes the records reveal the domestic arrangements of the keepers and their families. On the same day that full instructions were being issued as to the duties of the keeper, the Committee also ordered that a 'twin-up bedstead be provided for Bidston'. So, as well as rent-free accommodation, free coal and tools of the trade, such as a telescope, the keepers were even provided with furniture. By his first wife, William Urmson had four children – three daughters and a son. With his second wife, Ann, he had four more daughters. So, it's not surprising that in 1810 he petitioned for an extra bedroom for the accommodation of his family. A new bedroom was duly erected over the kitchen.

Although William Urmson was the Superior Officer of the Cheshire lighthouses it didn't stop him from getting into trouble. In 1814 the public signals, which informed the ship owners of the passage of their ships, were a major part of the Bidston keeper's duties and must have taken up a large portion of his day-time work. Urmson was instructed to take more care in the hoisting of the signals and he was given 'advice and directions regarding his future general conduct relating to the care of the Lighthouse and the general discharge of his duties'.

Urmson may have taken notice of these warnings for a time, but a few years later he was actually brought before the Dock Committee to be 'interrogated'. Again, the main cause of concern was the public signals. Having questioned Urmson the committee was still not satisfied that he was doing his job properly. He was therefore 'directed' to appear at the next meeting, but this time he had to bring along his journal containing his daily record of the signals hoisted. Very often the keepers devised ways to make some spare money on the side, and the hoisting of the signals was a case in point. Urmson was doing extra work privately. Only when he produced his journal, and assured the committee that, 'his attention to the private signals did not interfere with his duty to the Dock Trustees', was the situation finally resolved.

The Old Bidston Lighthouse & Signal Station.

Bidston was eventually to become part of the town of Birkenhead, but at this time it was still a small township. Even Birkenhead only had a population of 200 people in 1821, and William Laird did not begin shipbuilding on the banks of the Mersey for another three years. Nevertheless, Bidston must have had its share of lawbreakers, because windows were broken at the lighthouse by 'some person or persons using guns'. The culprits were never discovered.

As William Urmson's family grew up, they began to help with the day-to-day running of the lighthouse, especially his daughters Jane and Catherine, by his second wife Ann. The first mention of the girls is in 1827 when 'Miss Urmson' is paid £10 for 'superintending the cleaning of the New Lamps and Reflectors at the Leasowe Lighthouse'. As they were now all in their teens or early twenties £10 was a nice bonus.

## THE OWNER OF THE LAND

By 1827 things were changing, both on the domestic front and in the political machinations at the Dock Trust. The original agreement drawn up between the Trust and Mr Vyner, the owner of the land, had been for a sixty-year lease. Sir Robert Vyner had purchased the estate, which included Bidston Hill, in 1680. At the time Sir Robert was a wealthy banker and goldsmith. He had been Lord Mayor of London and was an important member of King Charles II's court and is also mentioned in the diary of Samuel Pepys. However, the title was not hereditary and by 1771 the estate was in the hands of Mr Thomas Vyner.

An interesting account of the Vyner dynasty[15] claims that in 1709 Thomas Vyner the elder was cheated out of the Bidston estate by his cousin, Thomas Vyner the younger. Be that as it may, the Vyners, in possession of the estate in 1827, were very keen to hold on to their lands; so much so that a long and protracted wrangle developed between the Dock Trust and the Vyners. The main stumbling block was the sixty-year lease. For ten years lengthy discussions took place about an extension to the lease or the outright purchase of the land. In sheer exasperation, Mr Vyner's bluff was called and the search for an alternative site began. Compulsory purchase was also suggested as a means to end the stalemate. Finally an intermediary, Mr Huskisson, was brought in to arbitrate and the land was sold, in 1827, to the Dock Trust for the princely sum of £10,260.

## WOMEN IN THE WORKPLACE

In 1826, the old signalling system, using flags and signal boards, was extended and a series of telegraph stations was put in place, stretching from Liverpool to Holyhead. Telegraph keepers were installed at each station, including the one at Bidston, which was separate from the lighthouse. Surprisingly, the Dock Trust was quite enlightened in its attitude towards women. Although it had insisted on Mrs

Wilding having her son-in-law to help her with the running of the lighthouse, it gave the job of the first Bidston telegraph keeper to William Urmson's daughter, Jane. She must have done a good job because, in July 1828, the following report was read out at a committee meeting:

> Lieutenant Watson [the instigator of the telegraph system] cannot avoid mentioning the very efficient manner which the Bidston Station is worked which from its contiguity to Liverpool has necessarily many more signals to attend to than any other Station.

Jane continued the good work and in 1833 her salary was increased to £50 per annum and in addition she was given £20 'for past services'.

With Jane installed as telegraph keeper, William Urmson's workload was considerably lightened. However, as he got older he found the duties of lighthouse keeper increasingly onerous. In fact, before he died in 1835, his two other daughters, Ann and Catherine, had been running the lighthouse for some time. The Marine Surveyor therefore had no hesitation in recommending the Urmson sisters, after the death of their father, to be joint lighthouse keepers at the same salary he had earned.

By the time William died, three of his children had predeceased him, including his only son. In his will, William left £235 to be divided between the three surviving daughters of his second marriage; Ann, Jane and Catherine, to 'share and share alike'. The value of his estate was less than Mrs Wilding's, but was still a reasonable amount. In fact, William Urmson had left his daughters something more valuable – a profession. With Jane as the telegraph keeper and Catherine and Ann running the lighthouse, these three women were carrying on the family tradition begun by their step-grandmother, Mrs Wilding.

Jane married Thomas Nichols in 1833 and they now ran the telegraph together. Catherine married in 1841, and from then on took no further part in the running of the lighthouse. Ann, however, continued as the lighthouse keeper. She too married in 1841, but this involved a certain amount of red tape. Because she lived at the lighthouse rent-free and it was part of her conditions of work, she had to write to her employers asking permission for her new husband, a cousin named John Urmson, to live at the lighthouse with her. Additionally, a 'certificate of his character' was supplied and Mr Urmson had to sign a 'Warrant of Ejectment to quit and deliver possession whenever required'.

For many years the Nichols and the Urmsons continued to work next door to each other on the hill. Unusually for Victorian times, the sisters did not have large families. Jane and Thomas only had one daughter, Mary Ann, while the Urmsons don't appear to have had any children. However, Mary Ann worked alongside her parents and eventually became the assistant telegraph keeper. She died when she was twenty-six, in 1861, and only three weeks later the Marine Surveyor reported upon 'the inefficiency from increasing age of the keepers of Bidston telegraph station' and jointly awarded Thomas and Jane a pension of £1 a week. So in the Nichols' case, the Dock Board treated husband and wife as equals. Seven

The lighthouse
as it was in
1841.

years after they retired, Jane Nichols died. Thomas Nichols was, by now, seventy-six years-old and 'in a very bad state of health'. Fortunately, the Dock Board decided to leave his pension at the same rate as he'd enjoyed while his wife was still alive.

Ann Urmson's case was different. She was still considered by the Dock Board to be the lighthouse keeper. Her husband obviously had a different view because he gave his occupation as 'lighthouse keeper' in the 1851 census and in 1861 as 'lighthouse keeper employing one man'. Ann was not credited by her husband as having any occupation but, in fact, he was dependent on his wife for an income and a home.

After Jane and Thomas Nicols had retired, the posts of lighthouse and telegraph keeper remained separate and the working routine continued. James Adams became the new telegraph keeper with his daughter Mary as his assistant and the Urmsons continued to run the lighthouse. In 1859 the *Royal Commission on Lights* visited Bidston lighthouse and noted:

> The house was moderately clean. The keeper was found to be a woman about 60 years
> of age, infirm, and by her own admission in weak health. She is assisted by her husband
> and niece. Her father kept the lighthouse before her. [16]

At the time, Ann Urmson was actually only fifty-five and she went on being the keeper for another ten years. When she died in 1869 the Dock Board seized the opportunity to make big changes. The jobs of lighthouse and telegraph keeper were amalgamated. James Adams became the keeper of the new combined service with two assistants, one of whom was his daughter Mary, and the other was John Urmson. So, twenty eight years after he moved into the lighthouse, Urmson was officially employed by the Dock Board.

Ann Urmsons' death marked the end of an era. The extended Wilding and Urmson families had kept the lights for over ninety years. Ann's involvement had lasted more than thirty five years, making her the longest serving woman lighthouse keeper at Liverpool's lighthouses. From 1869, until the lighthouse closed in 1913, there were seventeen different keepers working at Bidston. On average they only stayed for about seven years. With better roads and an expanding rail network it was much easier to move staff around than it had been in the earlier part of the century.

## INSPECTIONS, INDECISION & NEGLECT

During the 1860s and 70s the Dock Board held triennial inspections of their lighthouses, lightships, and other facilities. Not all the reports have survived, but the 1870 inspection reveals a catalogue of neglect. As early as 1861 the *Royal Commission on Lights and Beacons* commented on the poor state of the reflectors at Bidston, which were old and worn-out, comparing them unfavourably to the other lights in the Board's care. Nothing was done about it. It wasn't until three years later that repairs and additions to the lighthouse were approved – only to be countermanded by the Marine Committee during its triennial inspection of that year. They judged that more radical action was needed; both the telegraph and lighthouse stations should be remodelled. Other changes were also taking place on Bidston Hill.

At the beginning of 1863 the signal poles at the Bidston telegraph station were removed – the advent of the electric telegraph had made them obsolete. Only Mr Inman, ship owner, decided that he still needed his flag signals so they were allowed to remain. Today the holes which held the flag-poles can still be seen on the sandstone ridge. But as one striking feature disappeared it was replaced by an iconic symbol to the diversity of the port; a new observatory was rising alongside the lighthouse.

The original Liverpool observatory had been built by the Dock Committee at Waterloo Dock in 1845, but the Astronomer explained why the move was necessary and stated his requirements:

> With regard to the changes about to be made by the removal of the Observatory the offices and arrangements should, I think, be as near as possible to the landing stage, but the noise, smoke, and hot air from the steamers render such a position very unfavourable

for astronomical and meteorological observations. When the present building was erected we had not made the discovery that clocks could be controlled by electricity, and the Observatory was necessarily placed by the side of the time-ball and chronometer room, but there is no longer any necessity for this, as we can now control clocks and drop time-balls, at a considerable distance from the Observatory, with as much accuracy and certainty as though they were in the same building.[17]

Unfortunately, the new observatory seems to have distracted the Dock Board. Nothing was done in the lighthouse. In fact, to make things worse, the roof of the lighthouse was slightly damaged by fire in 1868. Luckily the fire was quickly put out, the roof temporarily repaired and the lighting apparatus was in order by 4.30 pm on the same day.

Things were slow to change at Bidston. In their 1870 report, the Board actually confessed that it had been *nine years* since the Royal Commission's adverse report. Not only had they taken no action to improve the lighthouse, but during the building of the observatory, 'some portions of the lighthouse buildings were pulled down, so that at present the whole establishment appears in a dilapidated condition'. The seriousness of the situation at Bidston was made all too clear as the report continued:

> This lighthouse, from its altitude, should in ordinary weather be the first of the Liverpool Lights to be sighted from seaward, and formerly was so, but the worn condition of the reflectors, the obsolete arrangements of the light room, and the defective state of the Lighthouse and Telegraph buildings, render it desirable that some conclusion should be arrived at, as to the renovation of this station.[18]

With the prospect of starting afresh, the Dock Committee looked at the possibility of powering the lights by the latest technology; either gas or electricity. The use of gas to illuminate the Liverpool lighthouses had been considered six years earlier when the Marine Surveyor visited the Bailey light at Howth in Ireland. Although it was agreed that gas-lit lighthouses had definite advantages, there were also disadvantages. Firstly, it would be necessary to change from catoptric to dioptric lights. The catoptric light was the original form, using a battery of oil lamps with reflectors, whereas a dioptric light used the modern system, which housed the light inside a cylindrical glass lens. Apart from the prohibitive outlay involved in changing the lights to dioptric, the catoptric lights had the advantage of a fail-safe facility – the loss of one lamp had minimal impact against the total loss of light if the dioptric failed. The possibility of using electricity was also considered, but rejected. At the time there were only two lighthouses in the south of England using electric light, but more were planned. Bidston, though, was so outdated and in such poor condition it definitely needed to be rebuilt and plans were drawn up for the new lighthouse and cottages.

*Right:* Old Bidston lighthouse, *c.*1866. (Reproduced with the permission of Williamson Art Gallery and Museum, Birkenhead; Wirral Museums Service).

*Below:* Plans for the new lighthouse and cottage apartments.

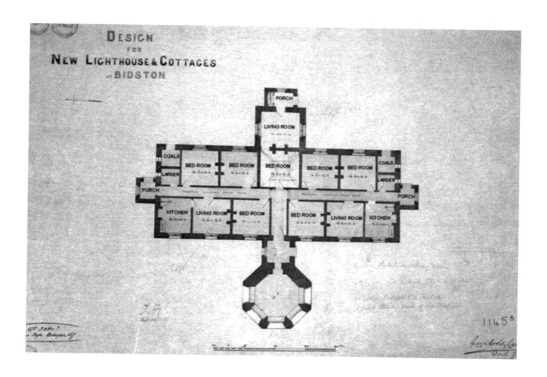

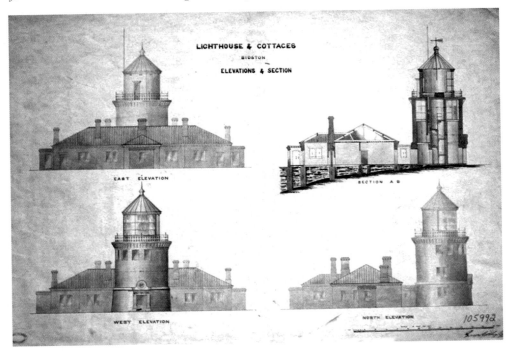

*Above:* The elevations and section of the new lighthouse.

*Left:* Stone Farm, the old Ring O'Bells, below Bidston Church.

*Opposite above:* Staircase leading to the lantern.

*Opposite below:* Bidston lighthouse and cottages.

Bidston lighthouse.

   With the old system one family, the Urmsons, looked after and lived at the lighthouse while the Nicholls' had separate accommodation at the telegraph station. Now, with the amalgamation of the two services, the Dock Board had the chance to rethink the living arrangements. In the plans (shown on p.57) the tower, costing £970, was linked to three cottages so a more traditional system of three keepers – two on and one off could be established. With a complete overhaul taking place it was decided to opt for the more expensive Chance Brothers dioptric oil light at an estimated cost of £1,600 with the panoramic lantern glazing costed separately at £250. The living accommodation, at £1,475, comprised two three-bed-roomed apartments either side of a one bed-roomed apartment with a living room, but no kitchen. This would have been for the third keeper; generally a single man who, presumably, ate with one or other of the two keepers and their families. So the total rebuild was estimated at £4,295. The light from the new tower was finally lit in 1873.
   Other changes had also taken place. The *Ring O'Bells* public house, just across the road from the church in Bidston village, had become so rowdy and

out of hand that Lady Cust, the owner of Leasowe Castle, petitioned Squire Vyner to have it closed down. He acquiesced, and so from 1868 Bidston was without a public house until a new estate was built on land adjoining the village in the 1960s.

By the end of the nineteenth century, Birkenhead's boundary had crept almost to the foot of Bidston Hill. Gradually the town was spreading towards the tiny village of Bidston. With the increase in Birkenhead's population, from 110 people in 1801 to almost 100,000 by 1891, came the need for more public open spaces. So, with money raised by public subscription Birkenhead Corporation bought forty-six acres of Bidston Hill.[19] Nevertheless, the village remained as it had been for centuries:

> It was a little, quiet, grey village – so very grey, indeed, and venerable, and quaint, that no flaunting red brick had dared to show itself and break the uniform tint of its gabled antiquity. The houses were grey, and the wall-fences were grey, and so was the church tower.[20]

Not surprisingly, the lighthouse became a visitor attraction and the Dock Board had to restrict numbers by instituting a permit system. In fact, visits to the lighthouse became so popular, that in the end they became a source of 'considerable annoyance and inconvenience', particularly on Sundays, so Sunday visiting was banned, unless an official order had been obtained.

That same year, 1894, Mr Jackson of Chester Street Mission School, Birkenhead applied for permission to take between seventy and eighty of the older children to visit the lighthouse. The children were allowed in, but only if they went in groups of no more than twelve. Visitors had to take particular care when entering the lantern, as the stairwell ceiling is so low. The incongruous protective material (in the photograph on p.59) is to protect the heads of today's visitors.

At the turn of the century the Cheshire lighthouses were phased-out. The first to close was Hoylake upper in 1886, followed by Hoylake lower and Leasowe in 1908. Bidston's days were numbered. New technology had made both the lighthouse and telegraph stations redundant; the former was replaced by lighted buoys in the channel whilst the latter had been superseded by the telephone. Alfred Morgan was Bidston's last keeper when it closed in 1913. He stayed on as caretaker until 1916 and then transferred to the North Wall lighthouse at Liverpool.

In 1918, Bidston lighthouse, the cottages and gardens were leased to Birkenhead Corporation for £50 a year on condition that the premises were only to be used by the employees who looked after Bidston Hill Recreation Ground.

As part of the Millennium Celebrations the building was renovated and a competition held to design a light for the lantern. Hilbre High school, West Kirby, won with a wind-powered design which was manufactured by the staff of Proudman Oceanographic Laboratory. So once again Bidston lighthouse is lit. At present the lighthouse is only open to the public on rare occasions and, just as in Victorian times, special permission is required to visit the lantern.

# 3
# Hoylake Upper & Hoylake Lower
## *The Lake Lights*

*Ordered that conveniences be made at the two Hoylake Lighthouses to enable the Keepers to Keep a Cow for the use of the Families at each Lighthouse.*

Minutes of the Dock Committee,
15 August 1815

The northern end of the Wirral Peninsula used to be divided into two ancient parishes: Wallasey, to the east and West Kirby, to the west. Before 1830 there were three sparsely populated townships along the north coast of West Kirby parish: Great Meols, whose eastern boundary just took in Mockbeggar (Leasowe) lighthouse; Little Meols, covering the western corner of north Wirral and between them the tiny township of Hoose (also known as Oolse or Hulse). In 1801, only 320 souls inhabited these three townships

Around 1830, Hoose evolved into the present-day Hoylake. But in 1764, when the first lighthouses were erected, the name 'Hoylake' was merely a shortened version of Hoyle Lake[1]. Only occasionally was it applied to the land on the shore of the lake[2]. According to parish records for the area, most of its small population lived off the land as 'husbandmen' or 'yeomen', but there can be little doubt that at least some would have used the safe waters of Hoyle Lake for fishing. Nevertheless, there were only two full-time fishermen recorded in the parish records during the 1760s, but the industry grew considerably in later years and there were many more by the end of that century.

In those days Hoyle Lake was crowded with ships[3]. These ships would have been transferring cargo, taking shelter or waiting for favourable winds. Because of the deep-sea shipping that used the lake, there had been a team of customs officers here since the seventeenth century. They were known as tide waiters and were led by the tide surveyor, who was under the control of the Collector of Customs in Liverpool.[4]

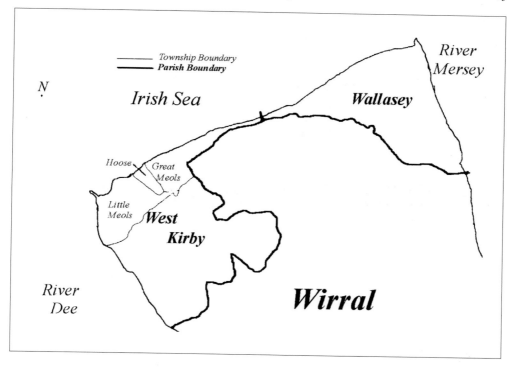

Map of West Kirby parish and its township boundaries, from the Tithe Maps. (Reproduced with permission from Cheshire and Chester Archive and Local Studies).

In the eighteenth century, a system of *pratique* was adopted that used a quarantine vessel or lazaretto (an old hulk moored in the lake). If a ship came in with disease on board, the sick were transferred to the lazaretto, where they would get better, or die. With plague raging in Constantinople in 1783, the masters of the pilot boats were warned to be careful when boarding vessels from the Mediterranean and to 'bring them into Hoyle Lake to perform Quarantine'.[5]

## THE FIRST LIGHTHOUSES

Erection of two lighthouses, known as the Lake Lights, was completed in 1764. Their purpose was to guide ships into the lake from the Horse Channel. The upper lighthouse was a brick tower sited about five hundred yards inland from the lower one. The latter was a portable wooden structure so that its position could be altered if necessary. Clouds of smoke billowed from huge coal fires, kept blazing in the lantern.

In 1764 the Dock Trust set up a special committee 'for settling the expense of Completing the Lighthouses' which was given many powers and responsibilities, including the following:

The old Hoylake Upper, 1836.

To issue 'rules and instructions to the receivers at Chester and Liverpoole; to the Inspectors at Hoyle Lake; to all masters of vessels coming into or going out of the Ports of Liverpoole and Chester and to the several Lightmen for the due observance of their duty'.

To appoint Jeremiah Ainsdell and Thomas Rimmer to be the first keepers of 'the Lights near Hoyle Lake' and to pay each of them eighteen pounds a year.

To employ Richard Gamon, the tide surveyor at Hoyle Lake, as an agent: 'not only to superintend the condition the Lights are kept in and the behaviour of the Watch or Light men, but more particularly to take an exact Account...of all Vessels Passing through the Lake ...'

After a couple of years the Hoylake keepers had a pay cut but the Mockbeggar keeper had his pay increased due to the extra hardship entailed at his lighthouse. This suggests that life at the Lake Lights was, at least in relative terms, something of a sinecure.

The first keepers of the Lake Lights were described as the men: 'who both inhabit in the Brick Lighthouse 70ft high at High lake and jointly tend that and the Low wooden Lighthouse'[6] There is no clear record of how long the first keepers remained at the Lake Lights, but John Smith, who was the keeper of the lower light for about forty years, started work there in the mid-1770s and Nicholas Seed was recorded as keeper of the upper lighthouse in 1776.

## MR HAMILTON'S REPORT

Unexpectedly, a detailed description of Hoylake's upper lighthouse, as it was in 1776, has survived in a document relating to another lighthouse in North Wales.[7]

In November 1775, the merchants and traders of Chester formed a committee with the task of improving the navigability of the approaches to the Dee.[8] This followed the wrecking of the brigs *Trevor* and *Nonpareil* in October that year. These two tragic events resulted in a total loss of 200 passengers and £46,000 worth of cargo.[9] The committee applied for an Act of Parliament that would enable them to erect two lighthouses on the Point of Ayr together with buoys and markers, on the North Wales coast 'so as to render the Passage in and out of the port more safe and commodious'. Liverpool Town Council's response to this was immediate as well as typical; they passed a resolution that opposed any such bill, because it would be 'detrimental to the Navigation of this town and Port'.

Nevertheless, having decided upon just one lighthouse for the Point of Ayr, the Chester men sent their secretary, Mr Hamilton, to Hoylake to compile a full report on the building and running costs of the brick lighthouse that had been erected there. In August 1776, Mr Hamilton's report was put before the Chester Committee. It contains a builder's estimate, based upon the construction costs of the Hoylake lighthouse, together with a revealing series of questions and answers. Some of the facts revealed in Hamilton's report are given below. (A full copy of the report appears in Appendix A).

### The Coal Light

1. Although William Hutchinson had enclosed the original open coal fire within a 'light room', it was still highly inefficient, due to the window being obscured with soot and impossible to keep at a regular brilliance. So, from 1771, it was replaced by an oil lamp.
2. When lit by coal the lamp consumed about five hundredweight per night, not including what was used for the kitchen fire.
3. The weather had to be kept out with a leaded wooden roof.
4. The work of carrying the coals to the top of the lighthouse and tending the fire was too much for one man to do effectively, and required the help of his family (or, as in the case of the Hoylake lighthouse, another keeper).

### The Oil Light

1. The light could be seen at a distance of twelve miles.
2. The diameter of its reflector was 3ft.
3. Only one lamp was used with a wick of 588 threads.
4. Three quarts and a pint (i.e. seven pints) of Spermaceti oil (from London) were used per night for the lamp and for two small lamps in the kitchen. This was about half the amount used by Mockbeggar light.
5. The lamp burned about ¾lb. of cotton per night.

### The Running Costs

1. The keeper, Nicholas Seed, received £16 per year plus £3.10s [£3.50] for coals for house use and a guinea [£1.05] every Christmas.
2. The total annual running cost was somewhat less than £165.
3. An annual rent of two guineas was paid to the Lord of the Manor.

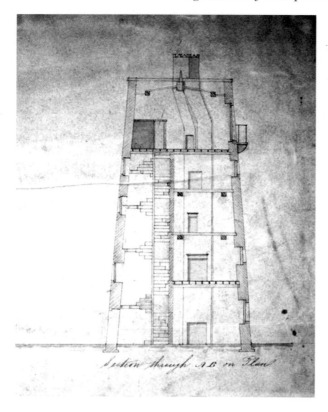

Section of the old Hoylake upper in 1836. Note the existence of a fireplace in each room.

## The Construction

1.  The lighthouse was about 55ft high.
2.  The foundations were set just below surface level on oak slabs and it stood 'exceeding well'.
3.  The landowner granted no land around the lighthouse except for the outbuildings.
4.  The bricks were made about two miles off; the timber, except for that of the roof, stairs and windows, was all deal and came from Liverpool. The lime was burned at Bidston Mills and the limestone came from Wales.
5.  The six stones for the balcony came from Upholland, Lancashire.

Mr Hamilton also noted: 'There are four Floors in the Hoylake lighthouse as two families live therein as they are oblig'd to take care of two lighthouses…'

The answer to one of the questions; 'What salary and what other allowances for attending the Hoylake light?' gives an insight into the keeper's conditions:

Nicholas Seed at the Hoylake Light, receives 16 pound in Cash, £3.10.0 for Costs for the house use, and a Guinea to his wife every Christmas if no complaint, Apartments to live, and a Stable and Shippon [*cow-shed*] for Cow and Horse; If it be lighted with Coals, the £3.10.0 is struck off, and the man takes Coals out of the Common Stock for House use.[10]

## FATHERS & SONS

We know, from Mr Hamilton's report, that Nicholas Seed was in charge of the upper Lake Light in 1776. He appears in West Kirby parish records in an entry for the baptism of his last child, a daughter, in 1774, as: 'Nicholas Seed, Mason, of Hoyle Lake'. In these early records, the term 'lighthouse keeper' was never used. Parish records show that they were sometimes called 'lamp lighters', or simply entered as 'of the lighthouse', while the early Dock Committee minutes referred to them as 'watch men' or 'light men'.

Some years later, Thomas, the son of Nicholas Seed, took over the upper lighthouse. He remained there until he died aged fifty-one in November 1808. A payment of £31 19s to a Thomas Seed is recorded in February 1808, 'for slating buildings at the Dockyard'. In his father's will, written in 1786, Thomas Seed is referred to as a 'stone mason' like his father. Perhaps the lighthouse job was merely a form of 'moonlighting' for men who plied other trades during the day.

Thomas appears never to have married and he didn't leave a will, but in May 1817 a maturing Dock Trust Bond is recorded, in the name of Thomas Seed, for the large sum of £500. It is tempting to string together odd bits of contemporary evidence, especially when they concern an unusual name but, nevertheless, another Thomas Seed may have worked for, and invested in, the Dock Trust at that time.

## MEANWHILE, AT THE LOWER LIGHT

John Smith, as stated earlier, became keeper of the lower lighthouse in the mid-1770s. He had married Elizabeth Linekar in 1763, who died in 1779, leaving him with six children. The youngest was just under two and his eldest daughter was fourteen. However, on 10 January 1780, John Smith 'of Hoylake Lighthouse' married Alice Clarke, 'a widow of this parish'. Smith and his family lived with the Seeds, thus it would appear that at least eleven shared the accommodation of the upper Hoylake lighthouse.

At last, in 1788 the portable wooden lighthouse was replaced with a brick tower. Messrs Waln and Foster, a bricklayer and a carpenter, did the actual building work, directed by a management team of four; two bailiffs, the dock treasurer and a Mr Case (possibly the Dock Surveyor).

When the new lighthouse was ready, John Smith and his family moved into their own home, by the beach of the Hoyle Lake. The design of the lighthouse was unusual, being a three-storey house with the tower incorporated at its seaward end. The outbuildings were similar to those that surrounded the upper lighthouse: a 'potatoe house', a 'pig house', a 'boiler house' and an oven. But inside, the main building was quite different. The spiral staircase was placed centrally. On the ground floor was a stable, kitchen and bedroom, with a privy and pantry attached. The second floor had a hayloft over the stable and two more bedrooms. The top floor had another bedroom at one end, with the 'light room' at the other. Each of the bedrooms had a fireplace, as can be seen on the section below.

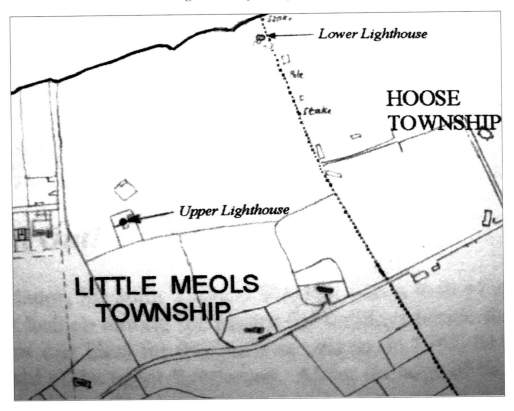

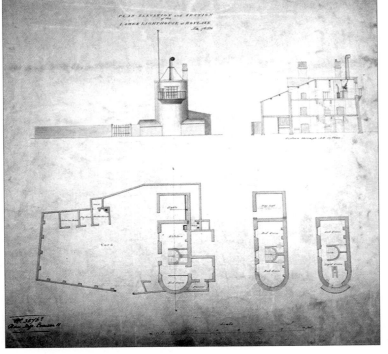

*Above:* Hoylake's lighthouses as they appear on the Tithe Maps of 1844. Reproduced with permission from Cheshire and Chester Archives and Local Studies

*Left:* The lower light, built in 1788, as it appears on a plan of 1836.

## PUT THAT LIGHT OUT!

The Lord of the Manor, Sir John Thomas Stanley, was a man of enterprise who was aware of the latest fashion among the gentry for holidays beside the sea. He decided that the Hoyle Lake was ideal for this purpose and so, in 1792, he built a hotel about half a mile westward of the upper lighthouse. Along the edge of the lake was placed a row of bathing machines. The hotel proved to be a success, but it was not popular with the Liverpool pilots, who complained of the 'considerable danger' caused by the lights from the hotel being mistaken for 'the Regular lights from the established lighthouses'. The Dock Committee petitioned Sir John:

> to Issue such directions to the Master of the Hotel, as will cause the Window shutters
> to the westward of the Building to be closed every evening immediately upon lighting
> of Fires or candles in any of the rooms on that side of the House, to prevent the Lives
> of our Seafaring Brethren as well as property of Mercantile Persons from being exposed
> to unnecessary Danger.

Sir John replied promptly, saying that the pilots' request: 'appears…to be founded upon principles of Humanity and general Philanthropy' and he assured them that in future the shutters would be secured each night. This appears to have put the matter to rest for eighteen years. Following several instances of shipwreck, caused by misleading lights from the hotel, another request was made 'that the Window shutters of the rooms which front the Sea be closed every evening immediately on the introduction of Fire or Candle lights.'

Appeal to the residents of the Hoyle-lake Hotel[11]. With the kind permission of the Liverpool Record Office, Liverpool Libraries.

*Above:* The old Royal Hotel, at one time the clubhouse of the Royal Liverpool, as it was in the 1950s. Unfortunately, it was demolished in 1958 to make way for houses.

*Left:* Hoyle Lake in the late nineteenth century with fishing boats and bathing huts.
'This shore is protected by a chain of sand-hills, held together by the star-grass or sea-reed…'[12]

In 1796 a visitor, staying at the recently opened Hoyle Lake Hotel, extolled the remarkable tranquillity of the Hoyle Lake, the pleasures of staying at the hotel and the sea view:

The Hoyle Sand breaks the force of the waves, so as to render the lake a safe road for vessels of any size in the roughest weather; and it is strictly true, that 'age and infirmity may securely plunge' during highest tides and most boisterous gales…The hotel lately erected by Sir John Stanley, the lord of the manor, is situated within a few yards of the beach, and contains a variety of commodious apartments, both public and private, very comfortably furnished. The charges are very moderate, the table well and amply supplied, and nothing is wanting on the part of the persons who have the management of it to render this house as pleasant and convenient as can be desired…Every vessel that comes into, or goes out of, the Dee or Mersey is distinctively seen hence; and the lake is frequently enlivened by brigs and schooners beating to windward, as well as by the anchorage of the Dublin packets, whose passengers are glad to partake of the amusements and refreshments which the hotel affords.[13]

From the 1830s onwards the patrons of the hotel had a grandstand view of the races that took place on the turf opposite. Much later this became the Royal Liverpool Golf Club's course, which has often hosted the British Open Golf Championship. But in the early days not everyone was quite so sure about the delights of the hotel's location. Ormerod wrote in 1819 that:

> …The erection of an excellent hotel…[has]…made this township of late years a place of resort for sea-bathing, notwithstanding an apparent dearth of attractions, situated as it is amongst a range of sand hills on the desolate extremity of a promontory.[14]

## INCREASED RESPONSIBILITIES

Compared to Leasowe, there were more job opportunities in Hoylake. Apart from the hotel and the customs station, a lifeboat was brought into service in 1803, providing extra income for the keepers and the fishermen. The dramatic scene at the top of the notice, on page 69, shows the Hoylake lifeboat returning from a shipwreck. The lifeboat station can be seen to the right of the lighthouse.

The tide surveyor, Mr Manlove, took charge of the lifeboat and was ordered to find a crew. Thus Thomas Seed, the keeper of the upper lighthouse, became master of the lifeboat, with John Smith, keeper of the lower light, as one of his crewmen. Thomas Seed died five years later and was temporarily replaced by his sister, Jane. The Dock Committee took the opportunity to introduce a rigorous new set of duties for the next keeper of the upper lighthouse, who had to be competent to take command of the lifeboat and responsible for its care and maintenance. Another duty for the new keeper was to act as 'constable', whereby he was accountable for the '…preservation and security of all property wrecked or driven on shore in Hoyle-lake,' as well as preventing the plundering of wrecks.

Joseph Bennett, a Liverpool pilot, was the ideal candidate. He was familiar with local conditions and had sea-going experience. Jane Seed had to vacate the lighthouse, for which she received a gratuity of five guineas (£5.25). Bennett's salary was agreed at £40 per annum, plus £10 from the pilots' Committee for reporting on 'the conduct of the pilots when upon the Hoyle Lake station'. In addition, as payment for his lifeboat responsibilities, he received ten guineas from the Liverpool Underwriters and ten pounds a year from the West India Association. The twelve lifeboat men received 3s (15p) for each call-out. Bennett's lifeboat duty included taking command of the boat whenever it was launched, whether for exercising the crew or attending a distressed vessel.

To make quite sure that Bennett would not have an idle moment, he was told that he must also carry out regular inspections at Mockbeggar (Leasowe) lighthouse and lower Hoylake; the former once a month and the latter at least once a week. Finally, he was reminded that he too would be overseen, when Captain Urmson, of Bidston visited all the lighthouses, including the two at Hoylake, and that Bennett was to consider Urmson his 'Superior Officer'.

Life at the lighthouses wasn't all hard graft. Bennett applied to have the ground floor of his lighthouse converted into 'a kitchen or a dwelling room'. Improvements to the quality of life continued, and the following year it was allowed that: 'conveniences be made at the two Hoylake lighthouses to enable the Keepers to keep a Cow for the use of the Families at each Lighthouse'. The Smiths at the lower lighthouse were even granted the luxury of a cast iron pump in place of the old bucket at the well.

By 1814, John Smith had been a member of the lifeboat crew for many years. At the age of eighty-three he asked to be retired. In view of his long service ('upwards of forty years'), his good conduct and great age, he was paid £15 a year out of the Docks Charitable Fund 'during the continuance of his life', which was, in fact, another six years. His son, John Smith Junior, aged forty-three, replaced him and held the job until he retired in 1836.

## LIFEBOAT TROUBLES

After John Smith Snr. retired, problems with the lifeboat surfaced. The Hoylake crew complained to the Dock Committee that they had not received payment for their lifeboat duties. On their behalf the Secretary wrote to the ship owners and masters demanding payment, and the errant ship owners duly paid up. The lifeboat men then asked for a formal system of payment to be instituted and that the Harbour Master, John Cummins, should act as their general agent, on 5 per cent commission. In addition, to avoid accusations of fraud, the lifeboat men would refer future claims to 'two competent merchants in this town'; one to be chosen by the Harbour Master and the other by the ship owner, master, or agent of the vessel that had been assisted.

The Hoylake lifeboat men were soon busy again, and remained so over the next seven years. Then, at 4 a.m. on 9 August 1821, the *Earl Moira*, a wooden sailing packet bound for Dublin, was driven onto Wharf Bank, near Burbo Bank, where she foundered and began breaking up. She had a general cargo and 110 passengers on board.[15] According to the log of the Hoylake lifeboat:

> The lifeboat-men began rescuing the passengers and saved 30, the others and the crew all being saved by a fishing boat from Hoylake and three boats from Liverpool[16].

In fact, the master, mate and between fifty and sixty passengers were drowned. A survivor's account of the scene at the shipwreck, together with his comments on the behaviour of some of the rescuers, makes grim reading:

> ...about half-past seven o'clock the life-boat from Hoylake was in view, and shortly after approached the wreck...When the crew of the life boat attached themselves to the wreck by throwing their grapple into the rigging, those sailors to whom the lives of the passengers were entrusted...being upon the top of the mast (by this time weighed down

nearly upon a level with the water), were the first to get on board her, leaving helpless females and weak men to shift for themselves: many plunged into the sea to gain her; some sunk to rise no more, and many were lost this way. It is solely to that cause, I attribute the conduct of the crew of the life boat in sheering off before they had taken near so many as they certainly might have done, nor have I the smallest doubt but more would be lost in making the experiment, than they could pick up by their best exertions. I saw some go down quite near her; some also returned to the wreck. While the life-boat was in view, several passengers, already weak and insensible, dropped from their hold and drifted off…Another boat now appeared in view…these were regular traders in saving lives, and made their bargain accordingly: after getting a few persons on board they sheered off. A second boat of the same description arrived about eight o'clock, and bargained in like manner, refusing to take any but those who paid largely, neither of them taking half the number they might have done. A fourth boat, belonging to Hoylake…behaved differently, taking all without any bargain, and using every exertion with great peril to take off the dying, which, with the assistance of another boat from Liverpool, and two brought out by the pilot boat, No. 11, they finally accomplished about half-past eight o'clock.[17]

Following the *Earl Moira* incident, the Secretary of the Dock Committee took the lifeboat crew to task, reminding them that they must act promptly and quickly when called out to a ship in distress and that they must land the survivors, or transfer them onto passing ships (where, hopefully, they would not be charged), so that the lifeboat could return to the shipwreck as soon as possible.

Joseph Bennett seems to have become less active, perhaps through old age, in the years following the *Earl Moira* incident. By the end of 1825 the whole of the lifeboat service, locally, had become moribund, so a special subcommittee was set up to deal with the problem. After a year a full report was produced.

A nineteenth-century Hoylake lifeboat on its launching wheels, with twelve crewmen and the master onboard.

This resulted in a new and improved lifeboat service that operated from points all around Liverpool Bay. Joseph Bennett remained keeper of the upper lighthouse until he died in 1828.

## GREAT CHANGES

Although working conditions at Hoylake were slow to change, a massive transformation was taking place off-shore; the Hoyle Lake was silting up and disappearing. This had been predicted many years previously by John MacKay, in his survey of 1732.[18] The first indication that this was happening came in September 1811, when the Dock Committee ordered that two beacons be put on Hilbre Island as leading lights through 'a remarkable good deep Channel in Hoylake called Hilbre Swash'. Hilbre Swash was a massive trench or gully, scoured out by altered tidal flows that were the direct result of land reclamations in the upper Dee estuary in the early 1700s. By 1811, the gully had cut straight across the great Hoyle Bank, dividing it into the East and West Hoyle Banks. Thus a bypass was forming for the mighty tidal currents that normally dredged the bottom of Hoyle Lake. Soon the old sea lake began to fill with sand and drain away [See appendix B].

In 1750 it had been said of the Hoyle Lake that it could hold all the ships of the British Navy,[19] and even as late as 1813 Daniel Defoe, in his *A Voyage Round Great Britain*, described the lake as: 'An admirable roadstead for ships of 600 tons burden'.[20] Yet in 1819, the Dock Committee had to respond to a rumour that the Lake Lights were of no further use. The Harbour Master was instructed to make enquiries and to report whether the lighthouses were still of value to mariners. The Pilots' Committee expressed alarm at the suggestion that they may lose the Hoylake lights. Under pressure from the pilots and the ship owners, it was decided that the lighthouses could not be dispensed with, even though the lake was now useful only to the local fishing vessels. The lake continued to silt up and in 1830 the lazaretto (quarantine vessel) was removed to Bromborough. Ten years later the Marine Surveyor, Captain Denham, said of the lake, '...at the present day we behold it a mere dyke 70 fathoms [140 yards] wide...2ft at its western end...and actually dry at its eastern'.[21]

## THE TIDE SURVEYOR

Bernard Sherwood, the son of a Norfolk farmer, began his career with HM Customs at Kings Lynn in 1820, but because Liverpool was growing so fast Sherwood was transferred there as a tide waiter in 1823. By 1828 he had been promoted to the position of tide surveyor of Hoylake. He also took over as superintendent of the lifeboat. From copies of his reports it is clear that Sherwood's customs work could be extremely taxing, particularly after storms had strewn the sand banks with shipwrecks. In a letter dated 10 February 1835, he describes how he and his men had to protect and gather-in cargo that had been washed ashore. His report begins:

> I beg to state during the 16 Days I was attending Cargo of the Within mentioned Vessel [unfortunately the ship's name is missing] I travelled along the Cheshire coast from the Red Stone Bank [*Red Rocks*] to the Magazines, a distance of 11 or 12 miles and the Cargo being washed up at so great a Distance I found it absolutely necessary to leave my Home for 12 successive Days & Nights for the protection of the Revenue.[22]

He finishes the letter with a subsistence claim for 'the twelve Days I took up my quarters at the Leasowe Castle'.

Mr Sherwood retired from the Customs Service in 1851. By then he had become an established and respected member of the community, and continued his duties as lifeboat superintendent. Many cases are recorded that show how hard he worked in the men's interests. For instance, in 1856 there was a fire in the roof of the upper Hoylake lighthouse which was extinguished without serious damage. Mr Sherwood obtained expenses for no less than nineteen men who claimed they had assisted in putting out the fire. They were awarded two shillings (10p) each for their services. On another occasion three Hoylake boats, with two men in each boat, retrieved a sunken buoy. Sherwood reported that the six men were out until 8 pm, so the men received a bonus of twenty shillings (£1) per boat. When Sherwood retired as lifeboat superintendent in 1864, Henry Bird, keeper of lower Hoylake lighthouse, took his place.

## New Lights for Old

When the recently formed Mersey Docks & Harbour Board took over from the Dock Trust their first major venture was to build a new lighthouse at Ormeshead. Once that was completed they turned their attention to Hoylake. Initially they were going to alter the lighthouse glazing so new, dioptric lights could be fitted in the lantern. After surveying the building the plan was changed. A new upper lighthouse and a house for the keeper were proposed and, at the same time, alterations submitted for the lower lighthouse. Only six months later the marine surveyor reported on the 'present dilapidated state of the lower lighthouse' and recommended that it too should be replaced. Presumably it had been pretty bad for some time, but the Dock Committee was often slow to react, as in the case of the neglect at Bidston lighthouse.

The estimated cost for the new lighthouses, including dioptric fixed bright lights, was £1,140 for the upper and £955 for the lower. These tenders were accepted, and by the summer of 1864 both towers were progressing steadily; the upper light was already 15ft above ground and the lower light a little less advanced. According to a Notice to Mariners, the new lights at Hoylake were exhibited on 8 August 1865, and the old lights discontinued and dismantled. Oddly, the date stone on the upper lighthouse reads 1866.

*Above:* Lord Stanley's sea wall and the new lower lighthouse.

*Left:* Inside the upper lighthouse tower.

Henry Bird and his family moved into the cottage at the lower lighthouse and James Lee junior took over at the upper lighthouse, with his wife and five children (the youngest just a baby). Bird was only able to enjoy family life at the lighthouse for another three years. Aged only forty-one he died in 1868, having served the Dock Board for twenty years. His wife, Margaret, was left with ten children. Her only assistance from the Dock Board was a one-off payment of £25 from the Charitable Trust Fund. James Lee stayed on at the upper lighthouse for a year before being moved to Ormeshead lighthouse. In 1868 J.E. Hughes, the keeper at upper Hoylake, was moved to the lower lighthouse and made superintendent of the lifeboat in place of Henry Bird.

## The Growing Town

At about the same time as the lighthouses were rebuilt a rail link between Birkenhead and Hoylake was established. There was great enthusiasm for this new form of transport which, it was hoped, would provide great entrepreneurial opportunities. Unfortunately, the route of the new line, Bidston, Moreton, Meols and Hoylake, was very sparsely populated with only about 2,000 people in the surrounding area.[23] Within three or four years the line ran into financial difficulties. The bailiffs moved in, the enterprise was shut down and Hoylake remained a sleepy backwater. No doubt the demise of the railway was good news for the stagecoach which had, for many years, run from Hoylake's Green Lodge Hotel to the Woodside ferry, Birkenhead.

A few years later, the railway was revived and a single track extended to West Kirby in 1878. Once the link to Hoylake was firmly re-established the village began its growth into a popular commuter town and seaside resort.

## The End of the Upper Light

Prior to its closure in 1886, Joseph Morgan was keeper of the Hoylake upper, along with Thomas Williams as assistant keeper. The families shared the accommodation. After it was discontinued, navigational aids, called the Dove Marks, were erected:

> They were rather weird diamond headed things, each with a pulley for hauling up a lamp …one was on the very edge of the sand hills, and was removed when the Meols promenade, or stone apron, was formed in the 1890s.[24]

Because it was an outdoor job, the keepers were each supplied with an overcoat, waterproof clothing and sea boots, in addition to their customary uniform clothing. They were also responsible for the care of the lamps and stores at the old lighthouse. After just four months of this new work, Joseph Morgan had had enough. He retired aged sixty-seven and Thomas Williams became the keeper, with William Kaney as his assistant. Finally, in June 1899, the Dove Marks were discontinued, having been made redundant by the use of the new gas buoys installed at Spencer's Spit. The keepers were redeployed, leaving the upper lighthouse empty.

The upper lighthouse was then let to Mr T. Walmsley with a string of conditions attached. At first the lighthouse apparatus was still in situ, so the rent was set at £52 10s per annum. Once the apparatus was removed, the rent was raised to £55 per annum. No reason is stated for the rise, but possibly the tenants were then able to have the use of the lantern room. No sub-letting was to be allowed without the Board's written permission. All alterations or additions to the premises had to be at Mr Walmsley's expense and he was also responsible for keeping the whole of the premises, including the tower, in good condition both inside and out.

The coach for
Woodside at the
Green Lodge
Hotel.

Hoylake
Promenade,
looking towards
the lower
lighthouse, *c.*1900.

This was quite an undertaking as the lighthouse was normally painted externally every two or three years. On the plus side, the premises were updated. The modernisation included a new kitchen range, but more importantly, a bathroom and toilet where the old kitchen had been. All told, the new work cost £55. After a year, Mr Walmsley's contract was renegotiated, greatly to his advantage, so that he was no longer responsible for the onerous and expensive job of painting the outside of the lighthouse. He was also fully insured by the Dock Board, against fire damage, storm or tempest and was allowed to sub-let the property, for three-monthly periods, without the Board's permission.

The upper lighthouse was spared the fate of the lower one. The lighthouse and the attached land were sold for £800 to Mr E.E. Wheeler. It is still standing in the grounds of a private house on Valentia Road. During the Second World War it was used as an observation post.

*Above:* Viewed from the
seaward side, with members of
the Association of Lighthouse
Keepers on a visit.

*Right:* Hoylake upper
lighthouse.

Hoylake lower lighthouse and keeper's cottage.

A pre–First World War postcard showing Hoylake's lower lighthouse used as the entrance to a concert hall.

Today the lighthouse commands fine views across Liverpool Bay, the Dee estuary and the Wirral, and is a valuable part of Hoylake's maritime history.

## THE LOWER LIGHT'S FINAL YEARS

Towards the end of 1892 there was an upset at the lower lighthouse when the assistant keepers both put in a complaint about treatment received from the principal keeper, Mr Askew. The Dock Board's response was swift and unusual: they moved and demoted Askew, making him first assistant keeper at Bidston lighthouse and reduced his salary by £10. He also lost the £10 a year he had been paid for acting as lifeboat superintendent. He was replaced by Bidston's first assistant keeper, William Kaney, who became the new lifeboat superintendent.

Hoylake's lower lighthouse continued operating until July 1908, when it was closed down along with Leasowe, leaving Bidston and New Brighton as the last of the Cheshire Lights. A year later both Hoylake lighthouses were sold. Mr C.B. Burrows bought the lower lighthouse for £936 10s. He used it as the entrance to a seaside concert hall called the Lighthouse Pavilion, which he built on the site of the keeper's cottage.[25] In 1920 the Pavilion entered a new era, as reported on 11 June in the *Hoylake & West Kirby Advertiser*:

> Several attempts have, in the past, been made with a view to improving the Lighthouse Pavilion, Hoylake, but never was anything accomplished that will bear comparison with what patrons will see on Monday evening. The old 'Lighthouse' [Pavilion] has passed away; at last the caterpillar has blossomed forth into a radiant butterfly. And now we have 'The Pavilion Super Cinema'. One's feet will sink into rich pile carpet; the theatre has a new white roof of elaborate design; the walls are artistically panelled; the seating accommodation leaves nothing to be desired; the whole place, in fact, has been conformed to the model of a first-rate modern theatre.

However, after two years it was obvious that even this project had failed. Sadly, in an attempt to remedy the situation the old lighthouse was demolished to make way for a new ballroom which, in the event, was never built. Because the old entrance (through the lighthouse) had been destroyed, a new one was built on Alderley Road and the theatre was then called the Winter Gardens. It became a cinema again from 1925. After a brief period as a 'live' theatre in 1930 it was reopened as a cinema with 'the very latest talkie installation' and so it continued until the 1990s, when it was demolished and replaced by private dwellings.

# 4

# New Brighton

## *The Black Rock Lighthouse*

*'…we have no information excepting from one or other of the keepers, and we generally find them very ready to give information against each other, for it is remarkable that they are generally on very bad terms; I know not how, but so it happens.'*
Alan Stevenson to a Select Committee in 1845

### 'A NEAT AND QUIET STATE'

The ancient parish of Wallasey lies in the north-east corner of the Wirral. With the Irish Sea to the north, the Mersey estuary to the east and the Wallasey Pool to the south and south-west, it was almost cut-off from the rest of Wirral. Added to that Bidston Moss, the low-lying ground to the south of Wallasey, was a vast tract of marshland with a few winding and uncertain paths crossing it towards Bidston. Thus, in the eighteenth century the only dry way out of the parish was via a coastal track that ran towards Leasowe Castle and the lighthouse between the sand hills.

Historically the parish of Wallasey was divided into three townships; Liscard, Poulton-cum-Seacombe and Wallasey. In 1581 there were said to be fifty-one families in the whole of Wallasey with a total population of 451.[1] By 1801 the population had increased to 663. Wallasey was the largest township with 274 people, Liscard had 211 and Seacombe was the least populated with 178. The area was a rural backwater mainly inhabited by farmers and those earning their living from the sea – boatmen, sailors, seamen and fishermen, along with the artisans who provided the backbone of the community such as tailors, millers, joiners and shoemakers.[2] Across the whole of Liscard there were only forty-three houses.[3] Even in 1847 Liscard was still an under-populated corner of the Wirral:

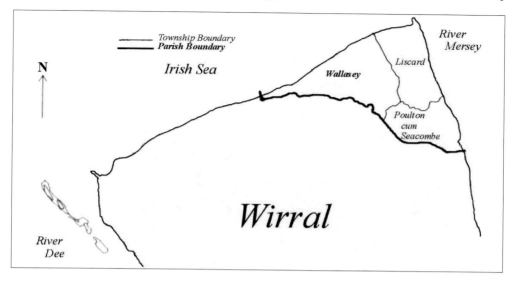

The ancient parish of Wallasey and its township boundaries, from the tithe maps. Reproduced with permission from Cheshire and Chester Archives and Local Studies.

> The ancient hamlet of Liscard has not kept pace with the improvements that distinguish most of the neighbourhood; it remains in that neat and quiet state in which it has been for many years, although there has been some slight increase even in the village. But in several parts of the township settlements have latterly been made, in which every effort of modern taste has been successfully used to add elegance to a district for which nature had previously done little. With the exception of the village, a few small hovels - the abode of fishermen and boatmen, and a range of low cottages, which from being used for storing gunpowder were distinguished by the name of 'The Magazines', Liscard was nearly a blank; there were not more than two or at most three respectable houses in the township.[4]

The 'respectable houses' included the old Liscard Manor House, which is now the Children's Library at Earlston Road[5]. The disreputable included a small public house known as Mother Redcap's – a reputed haunt of smugglers and wreckers. Built in 1595, it was converted in the nineteenth century into a mock-Tudor house, but was eventually demolished in 1974.

During the eighteenth century, armed vessels entering Liverpool were required to offload their gunpowder, which was then stored at a magazine in the centre of Liverpool. Although the quantity of gunpowder was not large, Liverpool Corporation thought it should be removed. Liscard was chosen for the new magazine because it was sparsely populated. Luckily for Liverpool, the move came at just the right time. After the transfer to Liscard, 'the trade in gunpowder Increased to a great extent'.[6] Eventually, as the population grew, in the mid-nineteenth century, the residents living nearby protested and the magazine was removed.[7] The gunpowder was then loaded onto floating magazines in the Mersey, 'but still within the port of Liverpool, and very near the town and shipping'[8].

Print of the Old Rock
Perch Beacon, Courtesy of
Wallasey Reference Library.

## THE NEED FOR A LIGHTHOUSE

As early as 1683 the Corporation of Liverpool had erected a primitive navigational
aid called a 'perch' to keep ships safe from the hazards of the Black Rock. The
'perch' was a simple arrangement; a strong pole surmounted by a triangular top
marking the preferred entrance into the river, the Rock Channel.

The Rock Perch beacon was frequently destroyed. The Corporation believed
it was 'wilfully and negligently done' and offered a reward of twenty guineas
to anyone finding the remnants of the beacon or information leading to the
conviction of the perpetrator. Normally, pieces of the wrecked beacon would
have been washed ashore, proving that the damage had been done by the sea. In
the absence of any wreckage vandalism seemed to be the cause. The explanation
is probably that the wreckers in Wallasey had been at work. An old rhyme
characterises the inhabitants of Wallasey thus:

> Wallasey for wreckers,
> Poulton for trees;
> Liscard for honest men,
> And Seacombe for thieves.[9]

By 1821 it was obvious that the perch was no longer sufficient for the needs
of the burgeoning port of Liverpool and moves were made for a lighthouse at
the entrance to the River Mersey. Before the Dock Trustees could proceed any
further, they had to apply to parliament for permission to build a new lighthouse.
Things did not move very quickly, and three years later the Trustees were still
trying to convince Liverpool Common Council that a new lighthouse was a good
idea. Finally the go-ahead was given in 1826.

While the lighthouse was being built, shipping still had to find its way in and out of the port; in particular prestigious enterprises such as the new Post Office Packet service which began in August 1826. Therefore the Post Master General requested a temporary light at the mouth of the river to aid navigation, which was granted. Apart from storms and sand banks, fog was often a hazard in the approaches to the port. Smoke from factory chimneys and thousands of coal fires combined with sea mists to produce the suffocating fogs which characterised the nineteenth and early twentieth centuries. The solution to the fog problem was to site a six-pounder gun on board the floating light vessel. When the Government Packets encountered fog they fired a gun. Answering fire would then be returned by the men on board the light vessel. With the Clean Air Act of the 1950s, the 'peasoupers' of earlier times are now a distant memory.

## BUILDING THE LIGHTHOUSE

The lighthouse at New Brighton is Liverpool's only rock lighthouse, standing on what is known as 'Black Rock' or 'The Rock'. During the nineteenth century the lighthouse was called either 'Black Rock', 'Perch Rock' or 'The Rock'. Originally it was about 200 metres below high-water mark, but was easily accessible at low tide:

> Built of Anglesey granite, the design incorporated an ingenious system whereby each block of stone was dovetailed, and each course of masonry fastened together with dowels and trenails. The structure was then covered with puzzolana, a type of volcanic ash, found at Puzzuoli, near Naples, which when mixed with mortar, formed a hydraulic cement that sets harder than the stone itself. The foundation stone was laid on 8th June 1827 by the Mayor of Liverpool, Thomas Littledale.[10]

This elegant structure is 90ft (27m) tall. The plans submitted by John Foster Junior, the Marine Surveyor, were based on the design of John Smeaton's Eddystone lighthouse. Smeaton's first premise was that the Eddystone tower must be built from stone. This would give it the strength needed to take the battering from the sea; but his inspiration for the shape came from nature:

> The English oak tree withstands the most violent weather conditions; so I visualise a new tower shaped like an oak. Why? Because the oak tree resists similar elemental pressures to those which wrecked the [Winstanley] lighthouse; an oak tree is broad at its base, curves inwards at its waist, and becomes narrower towards the top. We seldom hear of a mature oak being uprooted.[11]

It was a brilliant design. Robert Stevenson later refined it when he built the Bell Rock lighthouse off the east coast of Scotland.[12] Foster then, was following in the steps of the masters of lighthouse building. New Brighton lighthouse has witnessed many severe gales and hurricanes but it stands, unscathed, to this day.

Fort Perch Rock as it is seen today, with the lighthouse 'in the firing line'.

Once under way the building of the tower proceeded well. At the same time as it was being built, the neighbouring Fort Perch Rock was also taking shape. From 1758, when French privateers threatened the very existence of Liverpool shipping and the port, the Corporation had talked about erecting a battery at the entrance to the Mersey. The incursions of the privateer Paul Jones in 1778, at Whitehaven in Cumberland, only about eighty miles north of Liverpool, further concentrated the minds of the Liverpool councillors. Various temporary measures – batteries on the sand hills at Red Noses in Wallasey and one in front of St Nicholas' Church, Liverpool – were put in place. Eventually though, in 1825, the building of the fort began. It took four years to complete. The guns were only ever fired twice in anger – once in the First World War and once in the Second World War. On both occasions the vessels concerned were unaware that a war had begun and therefore didn't stop when challenged. Fortunately there were no casualties in either incident. Oddly, the lighthouse was built in front of the fort thus potentially placing it directly in the line of fire, in case of attack.

Resources were stretched with two major building projects in progress only a few metres from each other, plus new docks being built in Liverpool. To facilitate the movement of the stone to New Brighton from Liverpool, where it was being dressed and prepared, the loan of two 'flats' (small, flat-bottomed sailing vessels) was requested. The request was denied on the grounds that all the flats belonging to the Trust were wanted for the dock works. So a new flat, specifically for work on the lighthouse, was bought at a cost of £350, plus a further £250 for modifications. With the acquisition of a large shed and yard, for the preparation of the stone, the project finally began.

Accommodation at the building site and a place to store materials were urgently needed near the lighthouse. Mr Penkett, the lord of the manor, was applied to, and permission was given for the erection of temporary buildings on the upper part of the shore. The rent was set at 20s (£1) per annum for the use of the land.

By October 1827, after six months of work, five courses were in place and a halt was called while the builders waited for better weather in the spring. During the construction the work was repeatedly checked to make sure the mortar was sound and none of the courses had shifted. The stone was prepared and dressed in a yard at the north end of Princes dock where work continued through the winter.

Eighteen months later the building was far enough advanced for the Surveyor to go to London and order the lighting apparatus and all the machinery. The actual mechanism consisted of:

> a revolving horizontal apparatus with thirty reflectors and ten coloured glasses in order to exhibit at alternate periods a plain and coloured light and so arranged that each light will obtain its highest brilliancy every two minutes or oftener if required, and the whole to be ready for fixing in September next.

The cost of making the lighting apparatus and machinery was £2,300, which didn't include fixing or delivery. Messrs Robina & Wilkins, a London firm, the contractors used by Trinity Board, were chosen as suppliers. Although Liverpool was building its own lighthouses, Trinity House was consulted on various aspects. Their involvement became mandatory for all lighthouse decisions in 1836.

The exterior took two years to complete but, in June 1829 the Surveyor was able to report that 'the setting of the whole of the masonry of the Perch Rock lighthouse was completed'. For 'their attention and good conduct' the masons received a bonus of £3.

*New Brighton lighthouse* by W.G. Herdman. Reproduced with the kind permission of the Williamson Art Gallery and Museum, Birkenhead; Wirral Museums Service.

The masons and joiners were now able to work inside on the shutters, doors, staircase and fittings. After that the coppersmiths were engaged to fit a copper ladder which would complete the lighthouse, except for the lantern. Originally the railing of the gallery was also to be made of copper but in a last minute change cast iron was substituted. A month later the Chairman reported that the Black Rock Lighthouse had been satisfactorily inspected and the workmen were to be presented with the sum of £10. Finally, the Surveyor was able to announce in the *London Gazette* and other newspapers that the light would be exhibited on 1 March 1830. It was a red and white revolving light, visible for about thirteen miles.

## THE FIRST KEEPERS

At first there were only two keepers, whose working conditions were set out in a list of rules and regulations. There were two watches, sunset to midnight and midnight to sunrise. The men alternated between the first and second watch. Prior to the first watch, all the window shutters of the tower were closed to prevent light leakage. Throughout both shifts the lights had to be maintained at full power. This involved three-hourly trimming of the lamps, after which clean cylinders were fitted. Great care was needed in cleaning the reflectors; only fine cloths, polishing powder and leather skins were to be used. On no account should the light be allowed to go out and it should be kept burning at full power. The revolving machinery had to be kept fully wound and running correctly. At sunrise, the lamps had to be turned-off, all the lenses and reflectors cleaned, the oil reservoirs filled and generally the light made ready for the evening. A journal detailing the wind, weather and any important observations had to be kept. The daytime instructions mainly concerned keeping the entire lighting assembly spotlessly clean and the rest of the building in perfect order. In addition there were also storekeeping and clerical duties. During foggy weather the bell had to be rung every five minutes, day and night.

The first keepers were: principal keeper Samuel Appleton and second keeper John Williams. However, after three months a third keeper, William Flockheart, had to be taken on when it became clear that there was too much work for two men. At New Brighton there were twenty-two Argand lamps to look after. They consumed 1,033 gallons of oil per year. However, at Bidston, in contrast there were only eleven lamps. Handling this large amount of oil involved considerable logistical problems: its delivery, storage and use. The salaries were accordingly higher than at the other lighthouses – £100 p.a. for the principal keeper, £90 for the second keeper and £80 for the third keeper.

Black Rock was the only Liverpool lighthouse which had a traditional system of three male lighthouse keepers taking watches. All the other land-based lights were operated by families or couples. Unlike the usual rock lighthouse, the Black Rock is accessible every day when the tide is out. Therefore the men were free to go to their homes when not on duty.

The first New Brighton landing stage, *c.*1855. Reproduced courtesy of Wallasey Reference Library.

Surprisingly, Appleton chose to commute from his home in Liverpool. Today this would be a short drive through the Mersey Tunnel. For Appleton the journey from Liverpool to New Brighton would have been time-consuming. Firstly, he would have had to take a ferry to Egremont, followed by a two-mile walk to the lighthouse. Travel to New Brighton became easier in 1833 when a new direct ferry service from Liverpool was introduced. The journey normally took half an hour, but in stormy weather it could take a whole day. Either way it was hardly a comfortable trip. One of the boats used was the paddle steamer *Liverpool*, described as an 'awful old tub with cog wheels inside which rattled so much you could not hear yourself speak'[13].

## A Seaside Resort

Coincidentally, at the same time as the completion of the lighthouse, James Atherton, a wealthy businessman, purchased 140 acres of sandhills and heathland in the township of Liscard. He had looked out from his home in Everton across the Mersey with a view to developing the area. Atherton's vision was to change this rather bleak north-eastern corner of the Wirral into a resort to rival Brighton in the south; so he named it 'New Brighton'. He was not the only businessman to see the potential of the Wirral side of the Mersey. William Laird had already begun the process of transforming another sleepy backwater, Birkenhead, into a major town with the development of his shipbuilding business.

Atherton erected substantial villas along the sandstone ridge with magnificent views across Liverpool Bay. The villas were purchased by rich Liverpool merchants. For a while it seemed as if the new resort might indeed rival Brighton. Unfortunately, Atherton died before his plans could be fully implemented and the initial impetus was lost. The planned upmarket character of the resort was forgotten, and New Brighton eventually became a place for cheap family holidays and day-trippers.

Although there were comparatively few people living in the vicinity in 1830, the lighthouse seems to have been a tourist attraction from the start. So many people wanted to visit that admission tickets were issued. Authorisation for tickets, however, had to be given by the Mayor, the Surveyor or the Harbour Master, but only to such persons as were deemed 'advisable'. However, the Dock Committee deferred the issuing of tickets as the legal niceties regarding the management of the lighthouse had not yet been ironed out. This preoccupation with admission tickets seems to have stemmed from a scam run by the keepers. After a three-month probationary period the committee agreed that Appleton and Williams should be kept on, but they were not to admit anyone to the lighthouse without authorisation. They were also, 'prohibited from receiving money from visitors on pain of dismissal from their situations'.

## The Evils of Drink

Less than a year after the lighthouse was opened a perennial problem surfaced –alcohol and the excessive consumption of it. Williams, the second keeper, was dismissed for neglect of duty and drunkenness. One of the troubles with this posting was the ready access to what was known as 'The Devil's Nest'. Unfortunately, the temporary accommodation built for the builders soon became a haven for many disreputable characters. The Devil's Nest must have provided easy recreation and temptation for the keepers and, no doubt, for the young soldiers from the fort.

When Williams was sacked he lost a good job. Of the five Liverpool lighthouses then in operation – Lynas, Bidston, Leasowe and the two Hoylake lights – the salaries at Perch Rock were by far the highest. The Dock Trust must have had second thoughts about the salaries at the Rock, because later on the first keeper's salary was reduced from £100 to £90.

After Williams was dismissed, Flockheart was promoted from third to second keeper and Luke Johnson was appointed as third keeper. Thus a pattern emerged of one keeper after another either resigning or being dismissed. Flockheart soon resigned and then Luke Johnson was dismissed for negligence.

The replacement keepers were Matthew Curwen and John Christopherson. Like his predecessors it wasn't long before Curwen was hauled up and reprimanded for 'some neglect'. Only a month later, in October 1832, he was in trouble again, this time with Christopherson. Appleton, the principal keeper, reported them for being absent from the lighthouse when they were supposed to be on duty. Both were suspended for a week but then reinstated. However, they were reminded that there should always be two keepers on duty. Six weeks later Curwen was in trouble again for neglecting the light, but before he could be dismissed he tendered his resignation, which was accepted. On the same day as he resigned, Jane Urmson, the keeper of the Telegraph Station at Bidston, had her salary increased to £50 p.a. and was also presented with £20 for past services. The Trust must have been thankful that some of their employees were able to get on with their jobs without needing constant supervision.

## DENHAM TAKES CHARGE

For a year the keepers managed to stay out of trouble, but then Lt Denham, the Marine Surveyor, complained about the 'wanton neglect' of the first and second keepers 'in discontinuing the Tide Register'. They were reprimanded and 'ordered to pay the strictest attention in future and to comply with Denham's directions respecting the Tide Register'.

Lieutenant Henry Mangles Denham played a pivotal role in the development of the Port of Liverpool. He had been seconded from the Royal Navy to undertake a survey of the port and harbour. With the force of the tides in Liverpool Bay there is a constant shifting of sand which results in new sandbanks building up and the silting of channels which had previously been navigable. Denham reasoned that if one channel was closing another must be opening to release the huge volume of water. His survey successfully located the Crosby Channel, still used today to enter the River Mersey, then called the Victoria Channel.

*The Nest 1861, New Brighton Foreshore* a watercolour by H. Locke. Reproduced with the kind permission of the Williamson Art Gallery and Museum, Birkenhead; Wirral Museums Service..

Lieutenant Denham's skirmishes with Liverpool's tidal waters must have seemed easy compared to his battles with the keepers of the Rock lighthouse. Predictably, within a short time there was more trouble. This time keepers Christopherson and John Wallace were brought before the Committee. Christopherson was charged with neglecting the light for one hour. He escaped with a reprimand and a caution. Wallace, on the other hand, was dismissed for being intoxicated when he should have been on duty. Oddly, Christopherson seems to have taken umbrage at his treatment. He resigned but later returned and became principal keeper. Continual changes occurred until, rather bizarrely, Matthew Curwen was reinstated as third keeper!

Exasperated by unreliable keepers the Surveyor was 'instructed to make enquiry for a suitable family who would be willing to take charge of the Rock lighthouse'. This seemed like a good idea. The families who inhabited the other Liverpool lighthouses were, by and large, industrious and stable. Many were employed for decades with very few problems arising. Also the Dock Trust would, no doubt, have saved money. Instead of paying three men they would almost certainly only have paid the keeper and possibly an 'assistant'. In 1898, when Mrs Williams became keeper at Leasowe, her daughter Rose was only paid about £31 p.a. as her assistant.

Liverpool's other lighthouses all have good accommodation for families, but the interior of New Brighton lighthouse is cramped. Bearing in mind the clothes worn by Victorian women and the difficulties occasioned by the tide times, this would have been an arduous posting for a family. Add to that the dangers inherent with children and the idea was really a non-starter. Consequently the matter was never pursued and the lighthouse continued to be run by men.

The sectional drawing, below, shows the accommodation as it was when the lighthouse was being let as a honeymoon suite – a short-lived venture during the late 1970s. This pattern was probably based on the arrangements that existed when the lighthouse was in service.

Although the lighthouse is barely a few hundred metres from the shore, access is very difficult. Originally, there was a vertical climb up the fixed iron rungs before the door to the lighthouse was reached, 30ft (9m) from the rock. Nowadays, the ladder starts at high-water level to prevent unauthorised access. To get into the lighthouse, it is necessary to wade through a waist-deep moat. Then a wooden ladder has to be climbed to the base of the iron ladder, now about 12ft (4m) above the rocky base. Below the entrance, the lighthouse is a solid structure.

Once inside the tower there is an area where the stores would have been kept. Climbing up the spiral staircase leads to the storeroom. On the next floor, the kitchen is so small that the drop-leaf table has to accommodate the central 12in (30cm) weight-carrying tube that runs through the lighthouse. Many of the original fittings can still be seen: the fitted cupboards, the locker seats, which are divided into three compartments where the keepers could store their belongings, also the shuttered windows to prevent light seepage. The weight, which was wound up like a huge grandfather clock, was the driving force for the machinery that turned the light in the lantern. The lower lantern contains the lens clock and the upper level housed the optic.

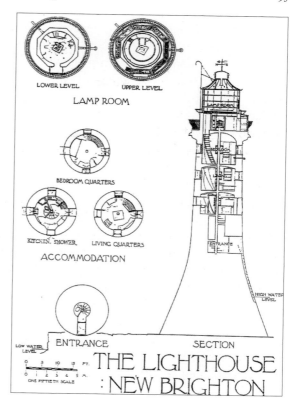

*Right:* A sectional view of New Brighton Lighthouse.

*Below:* The cramped living quarters with the central weight tube.

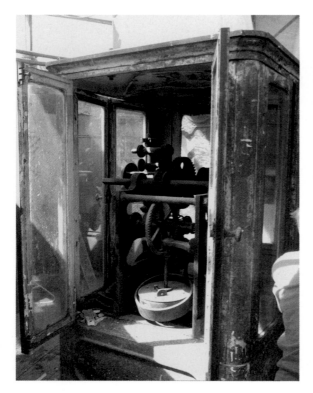

*Above:* A shuttered window.

*Left:* Lens clock and fog bell actuating mechanism. Made by Chance Bros, Birmingham.

## THE DESERTED LIGHTHOUSE

By the end of 1837 things seemed to have settled down somewhat, with Matthew Curwen now *senior* keeper and John Hannah second keeper. Being off-shore presented particular domestic problems which didn't occur at the other lighthouses. Water and coal were initially brought from Liverpool. Curwen suggested that both were readily available locally – water from a nearby spring, and coal from Seacombe. Economically this made sense and his suggestions were taken up. A year later, the Marine Surveyor advertised for:

> Parties willing to contract for carrying 28 gallons of spring water per week into the Rock lighthouse in quantities of not less than 4 gallons every day whilst the tide is out…The parties to live in New Brighton and find the jars or cans for carrying the same into the said lighthouse.[14]

After a period of calm there was yet more trouble. On a routine visit the Marine Surveyor found the lighthouse deserted. Although Curwen's explanation was unacceptable, he was merely warned that if it happened again he would be instantly dismissed. Undeterred, Curwen and his assistant Hughes were soon absent *again* and had allowed the light to go out. Both were reprimanded and cautioned. Curwen was also fined £5 (about three week's wages).

A few months later, Hughes was dismissed for permitting the 'Tide Ball to remain hoisted beyond its proper time…contrary to his instruction.' Not attending to the tide ball was a serious matter, but Hughes' earlier offence of letting the light go out should surely have been a case for dismissal. Really, the problem seems to be that although the Marine Surveyor was nominally in overall charge of the keepers, ultimately everything was decided by a committee which seemed hopelessly weak, allowing the men to break the rules time after time.

The tide ball was a large ball suspended above the lighthouse when the 'water in the shallowest part of the Rock Channel, the Rock Gut, was 12ft deep'.[15] Mariners relied on the ball as it showed there was sufficient depth for them to proceed. Even before the lighthouse was built the Rock Channel was the most popular route into the Mersey. This was eloquently described in the late eighteenth century:

> The eye being extended yet farther to the right [along the Wirral coast], reaches the most northern extremity of the Cheshire shore (a narrow point, called the Rock, round which every vessel passes, in coming in and going out of the harbour), and then becomes lost in the vast expanse of the Irish Sea.[16]

Although the vessel below seems very close to the lighthouse this is an accurate portrayal of the Rock Channel which was then in constant use.[17]

*Rounding the Perch Rock Lighthouse, Liverpool.* 1840, by Samuel Walters. Note that the tide ball can be seen above the lantern to the right. Picture reproduced from *Marine Art and Liverpool* by A.S. Davidson, with permission from the author.

Matthew Curwen's career also came to an abrupt end in August 1841, when he was suspended for 'neglect of duty and intoxication'. The Marine Surveyor wrote to the commanding officer of Fort Perch Rock requesting that he release George Brown, an artillery man, to give evidence before the Dock Committee against Curwen. Brown had seen him in a drunken state until late at night, when Curwen should have been on duty. The two other keepers were ordered not to allow Curwen into the lighthouse, pending the enquiry. His dismissal finally brought an end to *nine years* of complaints, cautions and threats against him.

Sometimes though, the keepers had a legitimate excuse for absence from the lighthouse. For instance, David Morgan, the keeper in 1841, was a married man with a young baby. When he heard that the baby was seriously ill, he left the lighthouse to be with his family. There was still one keeper on duty, but as two men were required at all times he was in breach of the rules; Morgan should have waited until he was relieved. Having explained his actions to his employer he then expressed his regret and promised there would be no repetition of the offence. Although he was not reprimanded he was obliged to obtain a medical certificate to prove his story. Presumably the Dock Committee had heard more than enough excuses from the Rock keepers.

On the other hand Thomas Stirzaker's case was completely different. Sea mists and fog are eternal problems at sea, so before radar and satellite communication were invented, a fog-horn or fog-bell were essential aids for mariners. At the Rock lighthouse three bells, each weighing 4cwt (20 kilos) were rung during foggy conditions. According to the *Rules and Regulations for Keepers*, Stirzaker, who was supposed to be on duty at the time, should have rung the bell every five minutes when it was foggy. This was not the case during the early hours of 20 March 1842.

When Captain Beazley, master of the steam packet *Queen Victoria,* entered the Rock Channel in dense fog and on a falling tide he found that the bells of the lighthouse were silent. Understandably annoyed, he wrote and complained. Stirzaker was summoned to appear before the Dock Committee with his log book. It was apparent that it had been altered. He was reprimanded by the Chairman for neglect of duty, also for the alteration which had been made and was cautioned as to his conduct in the future. When the fog bells were renewed in 1889 they were replaced by two bells weighing 8 cwt at a cost of £1,100. Each bell had a different note. They were hung outside the balcony and had to be sounded once every ten seconds.

## Change for the Better

Gradually things began to change, but occasionally difficulties could still arise. When John Hannah's young daughter died in 1853 he went home to be with his wife. He didn't leave the light unattended, but arranged for someone to take his place. Unfortunately the person chosen was not a Board employee. The keepers were therefore reminded that in an emergency they should arrange for one of their colleagues to cover for them.

The fog bell is on the left-hand side below the lantern.

Twenty-five years after the light was built, inspections still had to be carried out fortnightly. The main complaint was that the tower was dirty, untidy and neglected. Two years later at the triennial inspection there was some good news in that the lighting apparatus and machinery were in good order. However, the living accommodation was found to be less satisfactory, although it was acknowledged that the quarters were very confined. Even so the report concluded, things could have been better if the keepers had been more diligent about cleanliness.

It's hard to imagine how primitive the conditions were, but in practical terms it must have been very difficult to keep the place clean. Fresh water was at a premium. It was still being brought from a spring on the foreshore. Every single drop had to be carried in buckets, hauled up the outside of the tower and manhandled to where it was needed. Finally though, in 1870, the Rock lighthouse was given a favourable report when John Hannah and William Jones were commended for an improvement in the general state of the lighthouse. As well as painting the building the keepers had also made an effort to clean and tidy the whole of the tower.

At long last, in 1875, mains water was finally laid on. The pipe to the lighthouse was connected with the main at Fort Perch Rock at a cost of £110 for labour and an annual payment of £1 to the War Department. However, the pipe could be removed at any time if the Secretary of State for War demanded it.

Changes to working practices were also proposed. The new scheme meant that at New Brighton the men would receive the same pay and conditions as those employed in the lightship service. This meant that the senior keeper would become a 'subordinate mate' with three lightship seamen completing the crew. Historically, moving from a lightship to a lighthouse had always meant promotion, with the men becoming salaried officers once they were in the lighthouse service. Perhaps this change was an attempt to improve discipline at this particular lighthouse.

## A New Brighton Tragedy

Although not directly involved with the lifeboats, the keepers were witnesses to many shipwrecks and tragedies near the mouth of the Mersey. One such incident occurred in January 1883. The New Brighton lifeboat left the stage at around 2 a.m. and was towed to Crosby lightship by the tug *Black Prince*. Distress signals from a brig and barque had been reported by the lightship. The lifeboat searched for some time, but no more distress signals were sighted, so the ships could not be found in the darkness. In fact, one of the vessels, the *Star of Hope,* had been driven aground near Crosby where the crew managed to get ashore. The crew of the other vessel, a Russian ship, had also managed to get out of trouble. At about 5 a.m. the New Brighton lifeboat, unaware that both vessels were safe, was struck by a tremendous sea and two of the crew were washed overboard. One managed to catch a lifeline and was hauled back into the boat, but the other man, Charles Findley, was drowned. Findley, aged thirty-five, had been a stagehand on the New Brighton landing stage.

Although not a regular member of the lifeboat crew, he had volunteered to go out with the boat on this occasion. He left a wife and five children, ranging in age from one to twelve. Mrs Findley's mother also lived with the family. A report of the inquest summed up the findings:

> ...it was a most painful business...It was, of course, an accident of the purest kind, though of the most melancholy description possible. They could not speak too highly of the conduct of the crews of the lifeboats, who were a fine set of men, and were ready to face every danger in the interests of common humanity. He [the coroner] had not much under his control, but from the limited means at his command he would be glad to give £1 to the widow, with the hope that it might set the ball of sympathy rolling, which by-and-bye would result in some substantial help to the widow. The jury returned a verdict of 'accidental death', and subscribed 18s. 6d., which was handed to the captain [of the lifeboat] to give to Mrs Findley.[18]

After this, money poured in. Both the vicar of St James, New Brighton and St Stephen's, Liverpool, appealed on behalf of the widow. Reverend Vernon of St Stephen's, who had known Findley for over twenty years before be moved to New Brighton, wrote an eloquent epitaph. The Royal National Lifeboat Institution provided for the funeral expenses and the immediate needs of the family. Within eight days the people of Merseyside had raised almost £1,200 and the appeal was closed.

All donations collected were sent to, and administered by, the Liverpool Shipwreck and Humane Society. The Society decided that the best way to help Mrs Findley was to use the money for an annuity, rather than as a lump sum. She was paid £72 a year, reducing by £5 a year as each child reached the age of sixteen. On the death of her mother she would receive £10 a year less. By July 1914 there was still £222 left in the fund. The Society was set up on 9 January 1839, immediately following the disastrous 'Liverpool Hurricane' which caused immense damage and loss of life. Their objectives were set out in the form of an advertisement:

Liverpool Shipwreck and Humane Society
(Instituted 9 January 1839)

Chairman          Thomas Mills, Esq JP
Deputy Chairman   R. Stevenson Sandford, Esq

The Objects of the Society are:

First             To save human life, particularly in cases of shipwreck in the neighbourhood of Liverpool.

Second            To reward persons who have been instrumental in rescuing human life from danger, and to relieve the widows and orphans of those who have lost their lives while attempting to save others.

Third                    To relieve the immediate necessities of those rescued and to assist
                         them to proceed to their destination.

Fourth                   Generally to grant rewards and relief in deserving cases.


## A Popular Icon

With the colder winters of the nineteenth century, working conditions at the
lighthouse were particularly bad. In frosty weather for instance, condensation on
the glass had to be constantly cleared in order to keep the light shining brightly.
In 1890, the cold experienced by the men on duty was so bad at the Rock and
Hoylake lights that a 'hot-water heater apparatus' was installed. Perhaps the keepers
would have appreciated one of the 'wonderful oilskin coats' from Lewis's:

It is in the nature of things, that the 'nuisances' are always well-documented,
but often we know very little about the solid, reliable employees. One of these,
however, has come to light. His name was John Thompson Francis, who started
his service as a lightship seaman and gradually worked his way up to become
principal keeper. He served for twenty-seven years without ever getting into
trouble. At his funeral in 1902 there was a large gathering of family, friends and
local dignitaries, including the Marine Surveyor, Captain Bellam, the master of the
tender, *Vigilant*, and two of the keepers from Bidston lighthouse.


## A Day at the Sea Side

In its early days, the resort was nominally part of Liscard, but towards the end of the
century it had its own distinct identity. A contemporary account of New Brighton
was less than flattering: 'If the truth be told, we fancy that few readers would care to be
recommended to New Brighton, except Liverpool people.' The writer does concede
that the ferry service is 'first-rate' and 'the pier at New Brighton…affords fine views
of the shipping and docks of Liverpool, the Irish Sea, and the mountains of Wales'.[19]

Liverpudlians did indeed go to New Brighton for a day out. They packed the
ferry boats to capacity and the disembarking hordes crowded the beaches and
sand hills and, in later years, the promenade. Many strolled about the fort and
lighthouse. Families claimed their bit of the beach for a day-long camp in which
to laze in the sun, while their children played in the sand or paddled.

Gradually new attractions arrived on the once desolate beaches; donkey rides,
bathing machines and the notorious 'Ham and Egg Parade'. This was actually
called the Lower Parade and was lined with 'refreshment rooms' whose proprietors
tried to entice the unwary into them. Many people found it unsavoury and felt
that it gave New Brighton a sleazy image. Jerome K. Jerome, author of *Three Men
in a Boat*, visited New Brighton in 1894. He described his walk along the Ham
and Egg Parade thus:

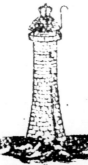

Advertisement from the *Liverpool Telegraph & Shipping Gazette*, 30 January 1884. Reproduced with the kind permission of the Liverpool Record Office, Liverpool Libraries

The gravestone of John Thompson Francis, principal keeper at Rock lighthouse.

New Brighton Pier *c.*1910.

Crowds on New Brighton beach *c.*1900.

In the course of some five hundred yards, I was stopped and accosted over a dozen times, and this in the middle of the afternoon; and in one or two cases I had to use some exertion to escape from the uninvited embraces of various ladies, who were anxious to inveigle me into what they called 'tea rooms'.[20]

This editorial, in Jerome's magazine *To-Day* provoked a lively response for the following month. Some pretended there was no problem, whilst others reaffirmed that 'They are simply a row of houses of ill-fame'. Jerome went on to say:

The correspondence that pours in upon me concerning what is locally known, I believe, as the "ham and eggs parade at New Brighton," puts the character of these tea-houses and their touts beyond all question...In no Continental city would such a state of things as exist at New Brighton be permitted for a moment.[21]

In spite of the bad publicity, it was more than fifteen years before the old Ham and Eggs Parade was swept away and replaced by the genteel Victoria Gardens, that day came in May 1913.

## 'A Marvellously Near Thing'

Over the years the keepers had witnessed many dramas. One of the strangest occurrences happened in 1921. Ferries taking holiday makers and day trippers ran regularly in and out of the Mersey, to Ireland, North Wales and the Isle of Man. On their return passages, they passed close to New Brighton lighthouse. At 1.30 on a foggy August afternoon, New Brighton beach was crowded with stoical summer visitors when, to their amazement, the Isle of Man steamer *King Orry* suddenly loomed out of the dense fog and ground to a shuddering halt. It ran onto a sand bank, very close to the rocks. The tide was rapidly going out and so the steamer, with her 1,300 passengers, settled firmly onto the beach. Immediately, a long queue formed outside the Marconi operators' room anxious to send wireless messages to relatives and friends. One of the passengers later told a reporter the vessel was travelling very slowly, when suddenly the lighthouse loomed up through the fog. 'How we missed the lighthouse, I don't know,' he said, 'It was a marvellously near thing.'[22]

The Wallasey ferry boat *Royal Daffodil*, the tenders, *Vigilant* and *Salvor* and the lifeboat all failed to get close enough to help, and by about four o'clock the *King Orry* was high and dry. Not long after, the first passenger climbed down one of the ship's ladders cheered on by the waiting crowd. By 6 o'clock the fire brigade had arrived with their wheeled escape ladders. Hundreds of onlookers watched as firemen assisted passengers in making a precarious descent to the beach. Around 1,000 people left the ship where a fleet of taxis, sent by the shipping company, took them to the bus, tram and train stations. The remaining 300 decided to stay on board. Eventually the ship floated off at eleven o'clock that night, watched by

*King Orry* aground at New Brighton. Reproduced from *Yesterday's Wirral* with permission of the author, Ian Boumphrey.

a huge crowd, and made her way back to Liverpool. There was no damage to the *King Orry* and she was back in service five days later.[23]

After ninety-four years of manned service, New Brighton lighthouse was converted into an unattended light on 8 December 1924, and the light was finally extinguished on 1 October 1973. The building is now privately owned and a small light flashes out, in Morse code, the names of 170 people lost on board the *Ocean Monarch* when she sank in Liverpool Bay in 1848.[24]

# 5
# Formby & Crosby
## *Liverpool's Lancashire Lighthouses*

*From reef and rock and skerry - over headland, ness, and voe -*
*The Coastwise Lights of England watch the ships of England go!*
Rudyard Kipling, The Coastwise Lights, 1896.

Formby and Crosby lighthouses, on the Lancashire coast to the north of Liverpool, were complementary lights: over a period of years they alternated, turn and turn about, as the shifting sandbanks dictated the need to change the position of the lights.

### FORMBY LIGHTHOUSE

The Liverpool merchants' decision not to build lighthouses in the seventeenth century left them with the problem of how to help ships find a safe passage into the Mersey. A partial solution was realised in 1719 by building an unlit brick landmark 120ft tall. It was situated on the east bank of the River Alt, at Formby.

Initially, it was used in conjunction with a wooden perch placed on the north bank of the Alt. This was later replaced by a 90ft brick landmark, near the sea's edge. Thus mariners could find the safe east-south-easterly course between the Mad Wharf and Burbo sandbanks, through the Formby Channel.[1] The position of the landmarks is shown on the chart below. By 1811, the lower landmark at Formby was in the wrong direction because the sandbanks had shifted, so it was replaced by another on a new alignment with the tall landmark.

Successful navigation of a sailing vessel through Formby Channel required great skill and experience, especially in foul weather conditions. However, any error on the part of the pilots was summarily dealt with by the pilot committee:

*Above left:* Formby and Crosby lighthouses.

*Above right:* Formby landmarks.

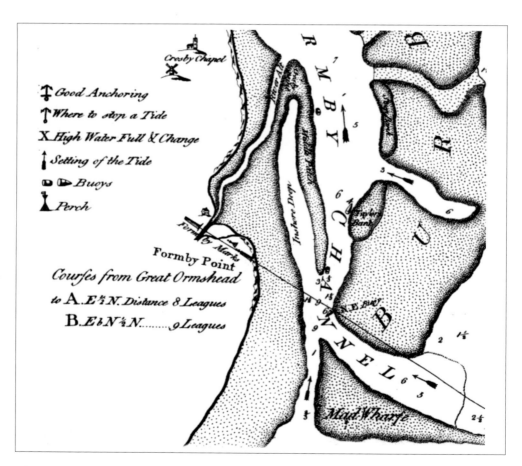

The entrance to the Formby Channel.

...At a meeting of the Pilot Committee held this 3<sup>rd</sup> day of Sept<sup>r</sup>, 1782 pursuant to adjournment...

Present

Jos.h Brooks Jun.<sup>r</sup>    Henry Koss

Wm Jenkinson Wm Hutchinson

Wm Denison  John Elsworthy

John Dirkins

Then appointed Jos.<sup>h</sup> Brooks Jun.<sup>r</sup> chairman and treasurer . . .

> Examined the complaint of Capt<sup>n</sup>. Graham of the ship Charles against John Cummins for running the ship on shore in Formby Channel by w<sup>ch</sup> misconduct the ship & cargo were almost totally lost.
>
> It appears that the accident was entirely [due] to the ignorance, wantonness & stupidity of the pilot. It is therefore ordered that John Cummins be deprived of his licence & that M<sup>r</sup> Lowndes do acquaint the impress officer of the said deprivation & devise him to take Cummins (if worth it) into His Majesty's Service.
>
> John Cummins inform'd the Committee that he lost his licence on board the Charles when on shore Mr Lowndes is therefore to give him notice that he is no longer a pilot. Ordered that boat No. 2 be stop'd from going to sea until Cummins's property in her is sold to some pilot or pilots.<sup>2</sup>

So, the three cardinal sins, according to the pilot committee, were 'ignorance, wantonness and stupidity'; poor Cummins! Perhaps he managed to redeem himself in His Majesty's navy.

## To Add Some Light

Inevitably the sandbanks shifted again, thus in 1833 a review of the navigation into Formby Channel was carried out by the marine surveyor, Lt Denham. He suggested that the tall landmark should be converted into a lighthouse and a lightship moored in the channel. This was agreed and a report drawn up itemising the costs involved. It contained the following estimates:

*For the proposed alteration to the landmark at Formby*

Expense of fitting up the present tower for a dwelling below, with a Staircase;

| | |
|---|---|
| and breaking out and securing the window for a light suppose | £300 |
| Lamps and reflectors | £400 |
| Total | £700 |

*Estimated annual charge*

| | |
|---|---|
| One man for attendance | £70 |
| Oil, cotton wick &c annual repairs | £100 |
| Total | £170 |

*Estimated cost of the Formby lightship*

| | |
|---|---|
| Cost of a vessel of about 100 tons bought for the purpose and fitted up | £1300 |
| Four anchors 12 cwt each…50 cwt @ 28s | £70 |
| Four chains 1¼ in 90 fathoms each with shackles about 280 cwt | £260 |
| One circular lantern with extra stores | £250 |
| Two boats with oars | £30 |
| Total | £1910 |

*Estimated annual charge*

| | |
|---|---|
| Three men £100 per year each finding themselves | £300 |
| Oil for one year, cotton wick & wear and tear, repairs &c | £150 |
| Total | £450 |

At only £700, the cost of converting the landmark into a lighthouse was considerably less than the light vessel. With only one man employed to look after the lighthouse, the running costs were not too onerous either. The keeper was to be paid £70 a year, while the three men on the lightship were paid £100 each. As in many early ships the men on the light vessel had to supply their own food 'each finding themselves'. In 1834 the tall brick tower at Formby was converted and, at 120ft, it became the tallest Liverpool lighthouse. The alignment of the lighthouse with the new Formby lightship gave mariners a safe course between the sandbanks.

Formby lighthouse.

## LT WALKER, RN

The first keeper of Formby lighthouse was Lt Joseph Walker, R.N. As well as being in charge of the lighthouse Walker was also responsible for supervising the Formby lifeboat, but he was under no obligation to go out with it. In 1777, the Dock Trust had had the foresight to install a lifeboat at Formby 'in readiness to fetch any ship-wrecked person from off of the banks'. This was arguably the first documented lifeboat in the world.[3]

Joseph Walker was a married man with three children. Unfortunately, not long after the family arrived at Formby, Mrs Walker died, so Lt Walker employed a young girl, Anne Bond, to take care of the children and help in the lighthouse.

In a letter to a local newspaper Denham graphically described the events which unfolded on 13 January 1836, after Lt Walker spotted a schooner in difficulty five miles north of the boathouse.[4] The keeper immediately hoisted the distress signal and fired the signal gun to alert the lifeboat crew. Before he left the lighthouse in the late afternoon, he told his servant, Anne Bond, to 'mind the light, and keep her eyes about'.[5]

When he arrived at the boat house, Lt Walker gathered together the crew and volunteered to go out with the men to the schooner *Bryades*. With the tide out, Gilbert Tyrer had to use his horses to drag the lifeboat three miles over the sand to the wild sea. Nevertheless, they were able to launch the lifeboat at 4 p.m., only an hour after the vessel was first sighted. Because the wind was too strong, the lifeboat's mast and sail had to be left behind in the boathouse, leaving the crew to row out to the stricken vessel. On reaching the schooner they found no-one on board, so they set off back towards the lighthouse through the cold and dark winter's night.

Over a hundred people had gathered on the beach waiting for the lifeboat's return, but, having almost reached safety, the boat capsized in the crashing surf. Three of the crew, Edward Alty, Edward Livesley and Henry Aindow, found themselves trapped under the boat. Alty managed to haul himself to the surface by grabbing one of the gunwale lifelines which had recently been fitted. He clung to the hull until the boat beached. Meanwhile, Livesley and Aindow, still under the boat, had found an air pocket. The oarsman's benches, being inverted, acted as rafters to cling onto as they were flung around in the surf. Hearing the moans from the battered and bruised men the people on the beach rushed forward to rescue them.

The rest of the crew; Lt Walker, John Brooks, Thomas Swift, Robert Formby and William Rimmer, all perished. Between them the men left a total of twenty eight children. In addition, Robert Formby's wife was pregnant and one of John Brooks' children was blind. Cruelly, Lt Walker's children became orphans.

The investigation into the disaster later revealed that the ill-fated endeavour had been completely unnecessary; the crew of the *Bryades* had abandoned ship, taken to their own boat and landed safely near Southport.

When the lifeboat was recovered it was found that all the gear was still on board, including the nine cork jackets which had been supplied to the men. None of the lifeboat crew had been wearing a jacket even though Cdr Denham[6] stated that he had specifically ordered that they should be kept in the lifeboat at all times. He went further than that, saying he had stressed that it was, 'my constant injunction to wear them fair or foul'.[7] On questioning the survivors, the only reason given for not wearing the jackets was that the men were so intent on launching the boat quickly that they simply forgot. Within a week of the disaster the lifeboat was again ready for use, and all three survivors volunteered to become part of the new crew. Denham recommended the three survivers and Gilbert Tyrer for a reward. He also singled out Anne Bond:

> ...for praiseworthily attending the lighthouse, amidst the conflicting scenes of a suddenly bereft family of children which, as servant to Mr Walker, she was called upon to sustain.[8]

The Marine Surveyor then went on, in his letter, to appeal to the people of Liverpool for financial help to alleviate the hardship of the families involved. The dock committee promised to donate money for the immediate relief of the families and also set up a fund to which the public could contribute. In addition, the Dock Committee awarded the widows of the crewmen two shillings (10p) a week for the rest of their lives – about £5 a year. Robert Formby's wife, Ellen, claimed this pension until 1898, when she died aged 104![9]

## The Great Storm

Joseph Walker's successor was the experienced John Christopherson who had been the keeper at Rock lighthouse. Christopherson was to play a major role in the controversy which, three years later, engulfed the tight-knit community in the aftermath of *The Great Storm* of 1839.

The British Isles is not often visited by hurricanes, but when it is, the results can be devastating. In the twentieth century, 1987 and 1953 both stand out for different reasons. The former was mostly land-based with large swathes of southern England bearing the brunt of the wind's force. However, the destruction of 1953 affected the whole of the country, and beyond to the Netherlands, wreaking havoc on land and sea with great loss of life and property. Similarly, the events which began in Ireland on Sunday 6 January 1839 were to affect many, on land and sea, in Britain and across the North Sea into Denmark. The effect on shipping across the Irish Sea, Liverpool Bay and the north-west was truly disastrous, but the events at Formby had repercussions which changed the lives of all those involved.

Sailing ships, which had been becalmed in Liverpool for some time before the hurricane, were finally able to set off on that fateful Sunday. The lucky ones managed to escape the full consequences of the fury about to be unleashed. Others ended up fighting for their lives and, in many cases, succumbing to the furious onslaught. The force of the hurricane began to be felt in Liverpool late on the Sunday evening. The leader writer of a local newspaper described his walk home thus:

> After leaving our office, which was just at midnight, the storm increased in violence. In going up Scotland Road, the writer was, particularly in passing the vacant spaces, repeatedly blown off the footwalk into the middle of the street, being wholly unable to hold his footing, so great was the force of the wind, which now blew from the southwest. As he advanced, the storm increased and, incredible as it may appear, he and a gentleman who accompanied him were forced along, at their utmost speed, by the force of the wind, in momentary danger of being thrown on their faces from the velocity with which they were made to run.[10]

By the early hours of Monday substantial damage had been done to buildings in Liverpool. Chimneys crashed through roofs, houses collapsed, trees were uprooted. Next morning it became clear that many vessels in Liverpool Bay were in trouble.

A major factor was that the north-west lightship, which should have been in place to mark the passage into the Mersey, had parted from her moorings on Monday morning. She had then left her station and put into Liverpool. The marker buoys had also come loose. Thus, vessels running for safety would have had to navigate the treacherous Burbo and Mad Wharf banks, relying on luck and their innate abilities as seamen. Bad enough on a calm, clear day, but at night, in the terrible ferocity of huge seas and tempestuous winds, it was a feat very few would dare to contemplate.

Just after lunchtime on Monday, John Christopherson sighted a vessel 'three or four miles southward of the lighthouse'.[11] Realising that the fore and main mast were gone, 'He hoisted the distress flag, fired the gun, and sent a messenger to the captain of the lifeboat to launch her immediately'.[12] He then rushed off to the lifeboat station only to find that the master of the lifeboat, Ralph Brooks, refused to launch the boat.

The next morning, Tuesday, at 8.30 a.m., Christopherson saw a vessel on Burbo Bank showing a distress signal. Again, he signalled to the lifeboat and set off for the boathouse. When he arrived he could see that there was also a brig stranded on the point of Mad Wharf. Thinking that the Magazines lifeboat, stationed on the Cheshire side of the River Mersey, was nearer to the ship on Burbo Bank and could probably deal with that one, the Formby lifeboat was launched to go to the aid of the brig on Mad Wharf.

The lifeboat's design was different from other lifeboats in the area, lying much lower in the water than was usual.[13] This design contributed to the calamitous events which unfolded as the strength of the storm increased. With the boat lying so low in the water little headway was made. After an hour it was waterlogged, so the men returned to the shore where they baled out. Once again they set off in an attempt to reach the brig.

Although the lifeboat crew tried desperately to reach the vessel, the *Harvest Home,* they were unsuccessful. Providentially, they were able to pick up the carpenter, John McLean, and another seaman who had been washed overboard from a small boat, and land them safely on Formby beach. By now the winter's night was closing in. The wind had eased somewhat but the sea was still boiling and churning with a heavy cross surf around the point of Mad Wharf. Christopherson and the two rescued seamen urged the lifeboat crew to go back to the *Harvest Home.* In view of the state of the sea and the approaching darkness the men refused. The keeper arranged with the lifeboat men to meet again at daybreak on the following day, Wednesday.

Nine men were still on the *Harvest Home*; the master, the first and second mates, the cook, three crewmen and two boys. With the ship listing and continually being swamped by the mountainous seas, all on board proceeded to climb the masts and lash themselves in the rigging to avoid being swept overboard. All that long day and night they continued to wait for the lifeboat to return:

> About twelve o'clock on Tuesday evening one of the boys died from the effects of cold and hunger;…the second mate, three men, and the other boy soon followed. At length the captain perished, about three o'clock on Wednesday morning, during a snow squall.[14]

The two survivors, the first mate and the cook, hung on grimly in the face of driving snowstorms, only to see other ships ignoring their plight as they strove to make the safety of Liverpool.

Meanwhile, the lifeboat crew was urged to make another attempt to rescue those still trapped on board. They refused. Bearing in mind that three of the crew were survivors from the earlier disaster of 1836, when five men had drowned, it is easy to see why they maintained that it was an impossible task. They reasoned that this time they would all be drowned if the boat was launched again.

Whilst the lifeboat crew was prevaricating, the owner of the *Harvest Home*, J. E. Blain, had taken matters into his own hands. He had made his way to Southport from Liverpool, a distance of almost twenty miles; not an easy journey at the best of times in those days, but, during that storm, quite an undertaking. On the Thursday morning Mr Blain managed to get together a boat and a volunteer crew and they rowed the eleven miles, against the wind, to his stricken ship. Only when they were in sight of the vessel did Blain see the Formby lifeboat put to sea and it was the crew of the lifeboat, in the end, who rescued the two survivors and recovered the bodies of Captain Kenn and two crewmen.

Mr Blain wrote a damning letter to the editor of the *Liverpool Journal* in which he stated that the carpenter and the seaman who had been saved on the Tuesday had pleaded with the lifeboat men to go back to the *Harvest Home.* The answer to the many entreaties made to them was, 'that they would not risk their lives to save others'. Mr Blain's anguish was heartfelt as he recounted the fate of Captain Kenn and the crew:

The steam tug *Victoria* & the Magazines lifeboat heading for the *St Andrew*

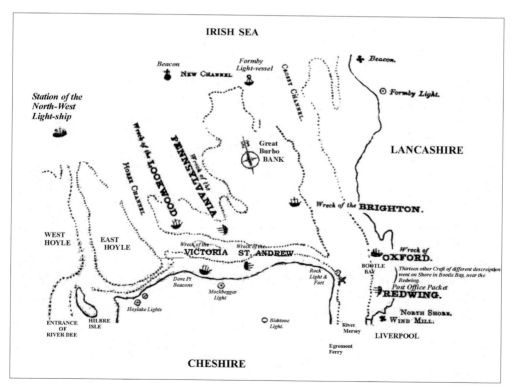

This wreck-chart indicates the positions of casualties of the Great Storm of 1839. It appeared in a special supplement to the *Liverpool Journal*, 19 January 1839. Reproduced with the kind permission of the Liverpool Record Office, Liverpool Libraries

These poor fellows were fifty hours in the rigging, and within one mile of the land at low water![15]

Many more ships and lives were lost over the three days of the hurricane, including the New York packet ships *Pennsylvania*, *St Andrew* and *Oxford*. Due to the scale of the disaster, the newspapers could barely cope with the information. Consequently, the contemporary chart, shown above, only includes the 'principal disasters' — those involving the largest vessels and those suffering the greatest loss of life. The *Lockwood*, taking emigrants to New York, suffered grievously. Of the one hundred and ten people on board, fifty-three perished, mostly from the extreme cold, but the steam tug *Victoria* was able to rescue fifty-seven of them. The *Brighton*, also shown on the chart, was the ship Christopherson saw on the Burbo Bank which he felt the Magazines lifeboat could reach. He was right. However, before the lifeboat reached the *Brighton,* fourteen of the crew made a raft, left the vessel and 'were never heard of more'.[16] The captain and the rest of the crew took to the rigging and were all rescued. The *Harvest Home* is not shown on the chart as she was wrecked further north.

With the level of criticism aimed at the lifeboat men and the crew of the lightship by, amongst others, Mr Blain, Christopherson and Commander Denham, an inquiry was inevitable. The actions of the north-west lightship and Formby lifeboat crews were examined. Some critics had condemned the lightship crew, saying they had deserted their station, but the report into the men's actions disagreed:

> ...the master and crew were justified in the course which they pursued...they did their duty to the utmost of their ability - keeping the vessel in her position as long as possible, and seeking her safety and their own when it became no longer practicable to maintain that position.[17]

On the other hand, the sub-committee hedged their bets on the actions of the Crosby lifeboat crew. They erred on the side of caution, ever mindful of what many of the men had experienced — either directly or indirectly — three years earlier. The committee had some difficulty in coming to a decisive conclusion on the subject of the crew's conduct. They also bore in mind that five men had drowned in the lifeboat tragedy of 1836, and that:

> The three men who were then rescued compose a part of the crew whose conduct is now under consideration; and it may be reasonably supposed that a feeling of greater caution must have prevailed amongst the whole of them, in consequence of that event.[18]

Nevertheless, the crew were censured in the final telling paragraph:

> If, however, some attempt had been made on the Tuesday afternoon, or on the Wednesday, such an attempt - even if unsuccessful - would have been more creditable to the life-boat's crew, and more congenial to the feelings of your sub-committee.[19]

*The New Custom House, Liverpool, 1845.*

During the three worst days of the tempest many had done their utmost to mitigate the shortcomings inherent at the port; in particular, the marine surveyor, Cdr. Denham. The wholesale devastation of shipping had galvanised him into action. Whilst the storm was increasing in magnitude Denham actually climbed up onto the roof of the newly completed custom house and 'from thence measured pretty well the devastation going on and to be anticipated'.[20] How he managed to hold on is difficult to understand, given the trouble some people had simply walking along the street.

Six months before the storm Denham had reported extensively on the silting up of the Rock and Formby channels. Mindful that 12,000 vessels a year were using the port, Denham had urged the dock committee to purchase a steam vessel for monitoring the channels. This would have been more effective than sail. The dock committee refused. Denham blamed the lack of a speedy, manoeuvrable vessel for his inability to sort out the problems caused by the hurricane. He needed to be where the action was.

During the storm, the lightship had parted from her moorings and the marker buoys had disappeared. Without the means of speedily attending to these problems Denham appeared to be helpless. It was not in his nature to remain idle. Eventually he managed to hire the steamer *Shamrock* from the Liverpool & Dublin Steam Packet Company and succeeded in towing the duplicate lightship into position and replacing some of the marker buoys. By then it was Wednesday and the worst of the storm was over.

Commander Denham's response to what he saw and experienced was to write a detailed account of his grievances both before and during the storm. He ended with an ultimatum stating the conditions which he felt were essential if he was to continue as marine surveyor. Denham offered to resign if his terms were not met. The dock committee replied by sacking him. It was Liverpool's loss.

Many honours came to Denham after he left Liverpool. Ironically, he was made a fellow of the Royal Society for his work at Liverpool, only a month after he was dismissed. He had a distinguished career in the Royal Navy and became an admiral in 1877. Denham was knighted for his work in and around Australia (where he had been sent), on board HMS *Herald,* to survey the waters around Port Jackson (Sydney).[21]

It is easy to take the view that the Dock Trust was in the wrong and Denham was right. However, the leader writer of the *Liverpool Albion* pointed out, in reference to those who said they knew there was a storm coming, that 'many people are wise after the event, and take instant credit to themselves for foresight'.[22] Perhaps, even with a designated steamer under his control, Commander Denham would not have been able to alter the course of events which had such catastrophic consequences in 1839.

After Denham's departure more changes were on the way. The newly discovered Victoria Channel was to be the new main entrance to the Mersey. Because of this, the light was removed from Formby lighthouse, which became a landmark again. Joseph Formby, master of the lifeboat, was employed as caretaker of the landmark on condition that he fired the gun and raised the distress flag whenever it was needed to summon the lifeboat crew.

## CROSBY LIGHTHOUSE

A suitable site was chosen for a new lighthouse and the landowner, Mr Blundell, agreed to a twenty-one year lease of about an acre. In fact, the quantity of land leased was very precise, being 100 yards long and 48½ yards wide. John Christopherson moved into the new Crosby lighthouse at the end of 1839. It was a timber structure near Crosby Point about a mile and a half away from Formby, at a bearing south-southwest along the Lancashire coast.

Naturally, with a wooden lighthouse, the committee was concerned about safety. General fire precautions were stressed early on in the planning stage. These included the specific requirement that the kitchen etc. should be built at a distance from the lighthouse in order to prevent the risk of fire. Paradoxically, it wasn't the wooden lighthouse that was destroyed by fire, but its brick-built replacement, sixty years on.

The transfer to the new lighthouse was Christopherson's third move. He had previously been keeper at the Rock and, of course, at Formby. Christopherson must have found living in the community somewhat uncomfortable. After all, he had publicly condemned the lifeboat crew, implying that they were guilty of cowardice during the great storm. Writing to Commander Denham, his anger is clearly evident. Christopherson ends his letter: 'The life boat's crew have behaved in a most disgraceful manner (with the exception of Edward Livesley)'.[23]

The original wooden lighthouse, 1840.

His belief in the culpability of the crew must have led to strained relations, not only with the lifeboat men, but also with the villagers. In any event, he tendered his resignation as keeper in September 1840 and doesn't appear to have been employed by the Dock Trust again.

Johnson Henderson thus became the new keeper of the lighthouse, but his tenure was brief, lasting only two years. On his death he was replaced by Thomas Stirzaker, one of the keepers at the Rock lighthouse, in September 1842. Like his predecessors, he was also superintendent of the lifeboat and crew. A measure of Crosby's isolation is evident in Stirzaker's request for the use of a pony. His reasons were twofold:

1. The distance from the lighthouse to the lifeboat was three miles.
2. The difficulty of relaying messages quickly and efficiently to and from Crosby or Formby lightships.

The sub-committee actually went to check the situation, even though they were in the habit of making regular inspections. They decided that a pony was necessary, and Stirzaker was given an allowance of £25 a year for its care.

Working conditions in the lighthouse were improved with the installation of a hot water system to warm the rooms. This was carried out by Jesse Hartley, the engineer, at a cost of around £75. Some things, however, were slow to change. In 1845 Stirzaker asked for three week's leave of absence in order to visit his friends. Nothing unusual in that, except that this was his first application for eleven years. Fortunately his request was granted and the committee agreed that a substitute should be sent to the light during his absence. Maybe the dock committee regretted their largess.

Artist's impression of the new Crosby lighthouse.

When David Morgan, the keeper at Point Lynas, asked for fourteen days leave a few years later, it was granted on the understanding that the expense of an assistant to fill his place was borne by him. After four years at Crosby, Stirzaker was promoted to be pier master of Clarence dock with a salary of £100 p.a. His previous salary, as keeper at Crosby, had been £84.

A year after the replacement keeper David Lloyd arrived at Crosby, navigation into the port changed again. Plans for a new lighthouse, half a mile from the old wooden one, were produced by Jesse Hartley. He designed a 75ft tapering brick tower topped with a wooden light room with an overall height of 96ft. The light first shone on 2 November 1847.

## FORMBY RELIT

David Lloyd's tenure was marked by a time of change. In 1851, after four years at Crosby, he was on the move once more; this time back to Formby lighthouse, as the sandbanks had again shifted.

Life at the reopened lighthouse appeared to go on quietly for the next four years, but on one of the marine surveyor's unannounced visits he found David Lloyd 'in a state of intoxication'. He was reprimanded and warned that a similar offence would result in his dismissal. Then the curse of Formby struck again on Christmas Eve 1855. David Lloyd was accidentally killed by an express train on the Southport railway. He was fifty-four and left a wife and two daughters aged fifteen and sixteen.[24] Lloyd's replacement was Thomas Abernethy, who kept the light at Formby for its last nine months. Then it was extinguished forever and Crosby was re-opened on Monday 6 October 1856.

## NOTICE TO MARINERS

*15<sup>th</sup> September, 1856*

Crosby lighthouse: – A light will be exhibited at Crosby lighthouse at sunset of the above date (Monday, October 6<sup>th</sup> 1856) and be continued every night from sunset to sunrise. The light will be stationary, of a red colour, elevated 96ft above the level of half-tide and be visible between the bearings of SSE ¼ E and E, which limits indicate respectively when a ship is westward of Formby Spit, or to the southward of the Crosby lightship. Formby old lighthouse. The light of this tower will be discontinued on the evening of the above date.

By order of the committee

Daniel Mason

secretary

Formby lighthouse stood as a reminder of times past for another eighty-five years, until the advent of the Second World War. When Liverpool and the docks became a prime target the lighthouse was deemed too great a help to incoming enemy aircraft. As a result it was blown up by the authorities in August 1941. By then the worst of the bombing was over, so Formby lighthouse might still have been standing to this day. In its short working life – less than ten years – Formby lighthouse was the scene of much misfortune. For the next forty years shipping along the Lancashire coast was protected by the lightships, buoys and Crosby lighthouse.

## BACK TO CROSBY

The new keeper at the reopened Crosby light, Thomas Abernethy, arrived with his wife and four young children, as well as his unmarried sister-in-law Mary, a dressmaker. When Abernethy moved, he asked if he could keep his garden at Formby. This was quite a distance away but he had a pony to help. Unfortunately, it turned out that the poor creature had become 'old and useless', having worked for the keepers for fifteen years. However, Abernethy was given permission to purchase a 'serviceable animal' at a cost of between £20 and £23 on condition that he carry the stores from Liverpool to the lighthouse and the lifeboat station.

During the dock board's triennial inspection of 1870, the possibility of using gas to power the Liverpool lights was considered. The argument put forward was particularly strong for Crosby where:

> …the light is subject to great disadvantages from its liability to be clouded by the smoke of Liverpool, [therefore] the arrangements for increasing the power of the light by means of gas would be peculiarly valuable…

In the end it was decided not to go ahead because of the cost involved in changing from a catoptric (several parabolic reflectors) to a dioptric (a single prismatic glass cover) system.

A watercolour of Jesse Hartley's 1847 Crosby lighthouse. Reproduced with permission from Merseyside Maritime Museum.

By 1881 Abernethy, his wife, his sister-in-law and two of his grown-up children were still at home. His son John had chosen not to follow in his father's footsteps and had become a clerk. However, lighthouse work usually required additional hands, often unpaid, so daughter Mary's occupation was given as 'keeper's daughter'.[25] It was Mary who was described, some years later, as the 'Grace Darling of Crosby'. At the end of the century a local newspaper looked back and gave the following account of the Abernethys:

Mr Abernethy and his brave daughter showed great intrepidity in succouring mariners in distress, and also were the means of saving lives before the lifeboat or other assistance could arrive. On one occasion, during a terrific storm, when there were no means of communicating to Liverpool and the lifeboat at the landing-stage the fact that a large vessel and its passengers were in a dangerous position and required help, Miss Abernethy, in the face of a severe storm, walked all the way from Crosby to the Liverpool landing-stage, [a distance of 10 miles] while her father, lamp in hand, walked up and down the beach at Crosby, giving what warning he could to those on board the vessel of the peril in which they were in. Miss Abernethy communicated to Mr John King, the master of the landing stage, who happened to be on duty, the fact that the vessel was in great danger in the channel off the Crosby shore. A lifeboat and tugboat were despatched, and what threatened to be a great shipping disaster was averted.[26]

On other occasions too, Thomas Abernethy was able to help ships in distress. For instance, in 1859 John McKee, master of the schooner *Liverpool* of Belfast, sent his 'thanks for kindness and hospitality…received from the keeper on the occasion of his vessel being stranded'. Three years later the keeper was rewarded for having saved the life of a seaman who was shipwrecked on Formby shore from the barque *Hindoo*.

In 1887 Thomas Abernethy died having spent thirty-one years at Crosby. He thus became its longest serving keeper and:

> … was known and highly respected on account of his arduous and oftentimes successful exertions in saving life by his bravery, supplemented by skilful and persevering efforts at resuscitation.[27]

Abernethy was replaced by Edward Jones who was both superintendent of the lifeboat and keeper for nearly ten years. Not long after he moved to Crosby, an incident took place that could have cost Edward Jones his life; fire in the lighthouse. Jones, his wife and a relative were able to put out the fire, which started at 6.30 a.m. At the time, the cause of the fire seems to have been attributed to the number of lamps in the lamp-room. Originally there had been seven lamps, but after this potentially life-threatening incident the number was reduced to five and more ventilation was put in place.[28] Jones retired in 1896, and Robert Buckley began his fateful tenure.

Even at the end of the nineteenth century the lighthouse was still very isolated. There were some buildings quite close by, including a few cottages, the Hightown hotel, a police station and, about a quarter of a mile away, the Hightown truant school. Not far away was Hightown station, taking passengers to Liverpool or Southport on the Lancashire and Yorkshire railway. The keepers had been part of this close-knit community for nearly sixty years.

## THE NIGHT OF THE FIRE

The position of Crosby lighthouse was bleak and exposed. Gales sweeping across the Irish Sea blew ferociously onto the unprotected low-lying coastline. At 96ft the lighthouse would have received the full force of the gale which struck on the evening of Tuesday 1 February 1898, and raged on until the next morning.

The mystery of what happened during the early hours of Wednesday 2 February would never be satisfactorily solved. The lurid headline in the *Liverpool Courier* set the scene for the tragedy which would dominate the local newspapers for many days:

TERRIBLE BURNING CALAMITY, CROSBY LIGHTHOUSE DESTROYED,
LOSS OF THREE LIVES, EXCITING SCENES

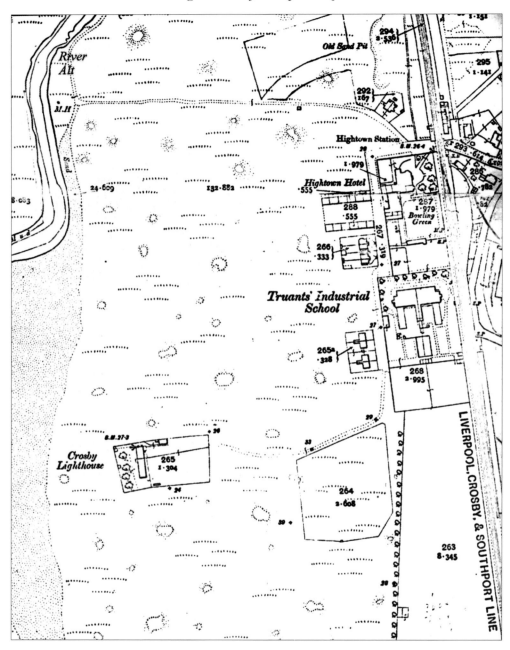

Map of Hightown, 1891. Reproduced with permission from Sefton Library Service.

PC Bond.

The first intimation of disaster came when a local railwayman, Thomas Bolton, arrived at his signal box at Hightown at 4 a.m. and saw two flashes. Realising that the lighthouse was burning furiously, he telephoned Crosby railway station and told them to call out the fire brigade. Then he sent for the village policeman, Constable Bond. As Bolton was on duty he had to stay at his signal box, so the policeman was the first person to arrive at the lighthouse.

As well as the tower, the lighthouse had a brick built house attached. It was quite substantial, comprising two storeys, with at least three rooms on the ground floor and three or four bedrooms above. Access from the house to the tower was through the sitting room. When PC Bond arrived:

> ...the tower was in flames from top to bottom. All the rooms on the ground floor were also in flames – at least the windows were lit up with the exception of the sitting room, which was in darkness. He broke the window of the sitting room and got in. There was no fire there, but on opening the door he found the hall in flames. He rushed out, and just as he got through the window the flagstaff from the tower fell at his feet.[29]

Constable Bond then ran about a quarter of a mile to Hightown station, where he and a porter grabbed a ladder and dashed back to the lighthouse. This time the policeman decided that Buckley and his wife might be trapped in the bedroom. Although the bedroom had not yet been engulfed by the flames, the uprights of the bedroom door were on fire. In spite of this PC Bond checked the room thoroughly; ascertaining that two people had been sleeping in the room but now it was deserted. A few minutes after he got out of the house the bedroom floor collapsed.

The lighthouse at the height of the fire, a drawing by Charles Lovelady, 1898.

Watching helplessly was the superintendent of the truant school, John Leech, who had been woken just after 5 a.m. by the constable. Mr Leech was called as a witness at the inquest but he also gave a graphic account of the events to the local newspaper. As the nearest building to the lighthouse, the truant school was at risk from the 'shower of burning sparks, which were being blown in a thick cloud by the heavy north-west gale which prevailed during the night.'[30]

With Hightown being such a small village there was no piped gas supply, so the gas for the school was stored 'in tins' alongside the building. Mr Leech continued:

> Having satisfied myself that all was safe with us, I hurried to the lighthouse. The lower portion of this structure was built of brick, the upper part, where the lamps and reflectors were situated, being of timber. I found the place burning from top to bottom, and I can compare the scene to nothing else than that which a huge furnace in full blast would present.[31]

When Crosby fire brigade arrived at half-past six, there was nothing they could do except watch the fire exhaust itself and prevent damage to the truant schools and railway buildings. Even if the fire tender had arrived sooner they would have faced an almost impossible situation. For a start the lighthouse was isolated across the sand hills, with no proper road leading to it. Also, the water supply was totally inadequate, consisting of a 1½in domestic service pipe. As the fire brigade arrived a series of small explosions occurred. They were either from the rockets used to signal to the lifeboat in times of distress, or from the oil in the lamps. The firemen did what they could:

The isolated, burned-out tower, Courtesy of National Museums of Liverpool (Merseyside Maritime Museum).

Pieces of charred and lighted timber were falling on the roof of the oil stores, and these a number of firemen were engaged in throwing off. They were told that there was something like a year's supply kept in the building.[32]

## THE AFTERMATH

The character of the keeper, Robert Buckley, and the actions of those involved, were pieced together after the fire. On Tuesday 1 February, Mr Buckley had been to the dock offices in Liverpool. There he discussed lighthouse business with Captain Belam, the marine surveyor, and picked up his wages. After that he caught the train back to Hightown in the afternoon and met Mrs Clements, his wife's friend. She had come to stay, partly because Mrs Buckley found Crosby lighthouse a rather lonely and isolated posting. Compared to Hoylake, which had become a fashionable seaside resort by the end of the nineteenth century, Hightown must have seemed a barren place, with nothing in the way of shops or entertainment. Mrs Alice Clements, a widow with no children, lived at Hoylake where she and the Buckleys had become friends. At that time Mr Buckley had been assistant keeper at the lower Hoylake lighthouse for five years, before being promoted to keeper at Crosby in 1896.

On the night of the fire, Mrs Buckley and Mrs Clements sat together enjoying each others company. Surprisingly, having already been out earlier in the day, the keeper did not join them but set off again to Liverpool just after six o'clock. The station master, in his evidence at the inquest, said that Buckley told him that he was going to take a flag into the stores. Later on that evening Buckley was seen at Hightown station getting off one of the late trains. The witness continued, 'He walked down the platform as if going to the lighthouse. He was perfectly sober'.[33]

According to Mr Horridge, for the dock board, on the night in question the lamps should have been lit at 4:54 p.m. Therefore, as pointed out by an inquest juror, it would appear that the lamps had not been checked for five or six hours after they were lit, because of Buckley's second trip to Liverpool.

After the fire. Picture courtesy of National Museums, Liverpool (Merseyside Maritime Museum).

Piecing together various scraps of information, the fire must have started before 3 a.m. on the Wednesday morning. Although the three people in the lighthouse were completely cremated by the ferocity of the fire there were various possessions found in the smouldering remains. Remarkably, considering the intensity of the heat, Mr Buckley's watch had survived but stopped at 3 o'clock. So, unless Mr Buckley had forgotten to wind up his watch, which doesn't seem likely, then it's reasonable to assume that the intensity of the fire had caused it to stop. This would mean that the fire probably started around 2 a.m.

The fire was seen for the first time by two different people: Thomas Bolton, the pointsman at Hightown station and, out at sea, the master of the Formby lightship, William Bird, who realised that the Crosby light was not lit. Just as he was about to phone the keeper to warn him, the lights came on, so he assumed Mr Buckley was trimming the lamps. However, after making himself a cup of coffee, he became aware that the light was too large to be natural and concluded it was on fire. Although he kept trying to get through to the lighthouse, there was no reply. Eventually he phoned Formby lifeboat station. They too tried to get in touch, but it was useless. By now the people in the lighthouse were beyond help.

The conflagration continued for many hours until the lighthouse and dwelling were reduced to a smouldering shell. There were so few remains of the three occupants that at first the coroner felt he could not hold an inquest. Subsequently, using what must have been the beginnings of forensic science, the police doctor was able to establish that three people had died in the fire. From the position of the bones it seems that Mrs Buckley and her friend Mrs Clements had died in the sitting room overcome by the smoke. What appeared to be the remains of Mr Buckley were found under the tower. However, the police doctor was cautious.

He could not categorically state that his findings were correct. He could only offer an opinion and not an absolute fact.

Trying to establish the exact cause of the fire was also problematic. Edward Jones, retired keeper, was called to give evidence. He roundly condemned Buckley. In his opinion it was:

> ...due to neglect of duty as much as anything. The man went out contrary to orders at half-past six, leaving the lamps to take their chance, and did not return until about half-past eleven o'clock.[34]

He also stated that if Buckley had cut corners and not trimmed and set the wicks properly there would be a flare-up, followed by an explosion.

Further testimony, from other witnesses, established that the lights were inspected regularly by Trinity House. The last inspection had been five months earlier, when 'the lantern, apparatus and the establishment generally were in excellent order'.[35] After the fire, the flash point of the oil used to light the lamps was checked and found to be well within the guidelines set by the government. For safety reasons the oil for the lighthouse was kept separate from the main buildings.

The marine surveyor explained the means of communication with the lighthouse. Buckley would have used the telegraph system if he wanted to get in touch with the dock office during the day or the landing stage at night. The telephone was in the kitchen but there was also a bell which rang in the bedroom. This meant that in the event of bad weather or shipwreck the keeper was directly connected to Formby lightship and the lifeboat. The marine surveyor further stated that the staircase of the lighthouse was made of wood and that:

> ... at the time the lighthouse was built (in 1847) that was the usual method of construction. They had had no complaint from Trinity House as to the construction of their lighthouses for a considerable number of years.[36]

Captain Belam also defined the keepers' duties. A record had to be kept of the temperature in the lantern; the highest recorded temperature being 92° Fahrenheit and the lowest 59° Fahrenheit. During the day the lighthouse had to be kept clean and tidy and the keeper had to answer the telephone perhaps two or three times a day. There was even a £5 allowance given for answering the telephone. Another basic rule stated that the keeper was not to leave the lighthouse after the lamps were lit unless he had written permission. Buckley did not have permission. At night, once the lamps were lit and sorted out, the keeper needed to check on them at intervals. The marine surveyor suggested what might happen if the lamps were not properly attended:

> ... the wick might flare up, break the cylinder of the lamp, and gradually the whole of the oil would be ignited.

But he was reluctant to commit himself fully. It *might* have happened in that way.

View from behind the five reflectors, showing their oil reservoirs. The curved stick in the middle is a dip-stick.

The *Illustrated London News* included an item on the catastrophe. Having mentioned the great gale that blew throughout the night of the fire, they suggested that:

> …the most natural explanation of the disaster is that the violence of the storm shattered the great lantern which has for so many years cast its five strong mirror-lights some twelve miles out to sea; and that the blowing in of the lantern led to the explosion of the lamps. The woodwork setting of the lights must then have caught fire, and the rapid spread of the flames downwards is ascribed to the dripping through of the burning oil from floor to floor.[37]

Included in the article is a picture of the lamp assembly used at Crosby.

The police tried to establish exactly what Buckley had been doing in Liverpool on that Tuesday evening, but they had not been able to trace his movements. No evidence was given that Buckley had been drinking whilst he was in town. Apart from Edward Jones, the previous keeper, no-one had a bad word to say about Mr Buckley. He was well known and liked in the village. Captain Belam described him as a thoroughly competent man. A friend who had stayed at the lighthouse only the week before the fire testified that whenever he was there Buckley regularly checked the lamps during the night.

The jury concluded that the remains of the people found in the lighthouse were Mr and Mrs Buckley and Mrs Clements, and that their deaths were accidental. A recommendation was added that if the lighthouse was rebuilt it should have all the latest safety changes; an assistant should be provided or proper measures should be taken to ensure that once the lamps were lit they were properly checked. However, the opinion of the pilot committee – that Crosby lighthouse was no longer needed – held sway and so its long history ended on the terrible night of the fire.

# 6
# Point Lynas Lighthouse
## *The Liverpool Pilots' Lighthouse*

*Anythin' for a quiet life, as the man said wen he took the sitivation at the lighthouse.*
Sam Weller in Charles Dickens' Pickwick Papers, 1837

Liverpool's main foreign trade during the eighteenth century developed into the infamous triangular route: outward, around the coast of Anglesey and south to West Africa, where goods were exchanged for slaves; then across to the Caribbean and the American colonies, where the slaves were sold to the plantation owners. Finally, homeward across the Atlantic, with sugar, coffee and rum from the West Indies; cotton and tobacco from Virginia. The route was then via the south of Ireland, up St George's Channel, around Anglesey's rocky coast and back into Liverpool Bay.

The Slave Trade, which peaked in the 1780s, was an integral part of Liverpool's growth into a leading seaport. The prospect of its abolition in 1807, so alarmed the merchants and councillors of Liverpool that they agreed to seek some form of compensation from the Government for its loss.[1]

### A SHELTERED HAVEN

Mersey-bound ships have picked up their pilot at Point Lynas, on the north-eastern tip of Anglesey, since 1781. Two years earlier, four Liverpool men, including William Hutchinson, the dock master, had set off on horse-back for the two-day journey to Anglesey. Their objective was to find a suitable place for a new pilot station. Moelfre was found unacceptable because of a troublesome gravel bar. That evening, the remoteness of the area became apparent: 'After spending the day here, we were obliged to ride seven miles into the country, to get accommodation for ourselves and horses.'[2]

'Appearance of Point Lynas and its Lighthouse when nearing it from the Westward'[3].

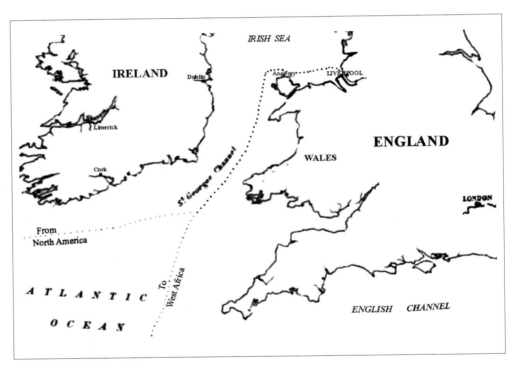

The Western Approaches from the Atlantic into the Irish Sea.

The next day they tried 'Hemlock' (Amlwch) and Bull Bay, but, these too, were rejected. Finally, they came to Point Lynas, a small peninsula running northwards with sheltered bays on either side. Over the next two days, the headland and bays of Point Lynas were surveyed. Happy with the result, Hutchinson and his colleagues celebrated their discovery:

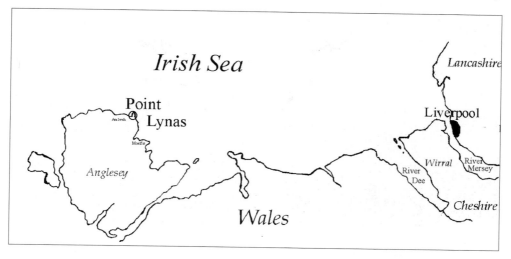

The positions of Point Lynas and Liverpool.

> We had ale brought and drank success to "Pilots' Harbour", which all the neighbourhood, great and small, seemed to be well wishers to its going forward.[4]

The map of Lynas Point drawn at the time has survived. It has the following explanatory notes and numbers:

References on A Plan of Elynus Point in the Island of Anglesea.

1.  The cut or slip for the rowing boats to be hove up and launch'd down occasionally.
2   A crab for heaving up the boats into the slip.
3.  The pilots house.
4.  A smithy
5-5. A piece of ground 200 yards from 5 to 5 rented by the Corporation of Liverpool.
6.  A road of 15 yards broad for H. Morgan, esq. to go the point 7.
8-8. A road of 15 yards broad to go from the piece of land marked 5.5 into the country.
9.  The Pilots' Harbour.
10. An island or a rock belonging to Bennett Williams, esq.
11. A fine shelly beach from which large stones have carried up on the rocky side
12. The rocky side.
13. Low water mark.
14. Brooks of fresh water.

Leased to the Corporation for 21 years from September 1779 at £10 per an. rent.

Once the site had been chosen, a small plot of land was leased from Henry Morgan and a watchhouse erected to accommodate the pilots. It was painted

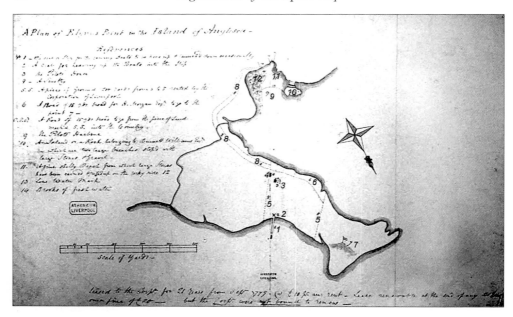

Pen & ink drawing of Point Lynas, 1780. The numbering on the chart has been enhanced by the authors. Reproduced by the kind permission of the Athenaeum, Liverpool.

white and provided with a flag pole for signalling. Inside, a rudimentary lighthouse was established comprising two small reflector lamps that shone out of the upper windows, one faced north-west and the other east. Below the headland pilots used the sheltered waters to join and depart from ships.

Typically, Hutchinson and the Pilot Committee laid down clear and precise instructions on the safe use of the new installation:

> All Ships and Vessels wanting Pilots for Liverpool and the adjacent Ports may steer boldly
> for this Point, hoist their Colours by day and shew Lights or fire guns by Night, and run
> close in Shore and bring too, either in Williams or Pilots Bay…according to the Winds,
> that they be boarded in smooth water with the greater safety both to themselves and
> Pilots…[5]

The lights were not visible to seaward, but 'only upon the longshore aspects'.[6] Thus they were leading lights into one or the other of the bays on either side of the Point.

At first, the pilots used the building to live in as they waited to board Liverpool-bound vessels on the last fifty miles of their voyage. Moorings were also laid in the bays and a six-oared boat was kept at a nearby slip. When a vessel had been signalled to enter and moor in the sheltered bay, the pilot was taken out to her. By 1796, eight large pilot boats were in use on the approaches to Liverpool and it appears that the house on Lynas Point no longer accommodated pilots, but was used only as a simple lighthouse.

The name 'Point Lynas' is one of many used for the headland. Others included: Hillary, Eleanus, Aelianus, Aelynus, Elynus, Eilian and Lynus. In 1899 the Ordnance Survey Office asked the Dock Board for the correct name of the peninsula for their revised maps. In the first edition of the map the name was spelled 'Point Aelianus'. The Dock Board replied that it was now called 'Point Lynas'. In fact, on the current Ordnance Survey map the name is given both in English as Point Lynas and in Welsh as Trwyn Eilian.

## THE FIRST KEEPER

The first recorded keeper of the lights was Robert Beaver. Born in 1748, he had gone to sea at an early age and eventually commanded a Liverpool slave-trader. Later he became captain of a privateer – an armed merchant ship that held a government licence to attack French and American ships. By the time Beaver left the sea, in 1782, his health had deteriorated, no doubt due to the years spent on the West African Coast and in the Caribbean. He is reputed to have taken many 'prizes' (successful captures of ships) during his years as a privateer captain.[7]

Beaver started his work as 'governor of the lighthouse' around 1787. In 1793, he complained that the building was in 'extreme want of repair' but that it was impossible to get anyone to do the work, so men had to be sent out to Anglesey, from Liverpool, to carry out the necessary repairs. Beaver had retired from the sea as quite a rich man, but in 1797 he petitioned the Pilot Committee for 'some allowance to be made to him annually' on the grounds that he had, for many years, worked for the pilots without any payment. It was agreed to pay him a salary of £25 per year, plus free coal, delivered by the pilots, as had been done previously.

In 1801, Robert Stevenson briefly included Lynas in his description of the Liverpool lighthouses:

> Besides these [the four 'Cheshire Lights'] there is a fifth light (supported by the Trade of Liverpool), namely, Lynas, in the island of Anglesey, to direct vessels into Beaumaris Bay when put past Liverpool and the Lake roads, but this small light is in use only during the winter months.[8]

It is perhaps surprising that Stevenson found Lynas to be a winter-only light, as Robert Beaver was being paid an annual keeper's salary and the pilots provided a year-round service.

In addition to his main job Beaver worked for the Royal Navy keeping a lookout for invading American or French warships, but in 1805 he was relieved of this extra duty when the Navy sent their own man, Lieutenant Robert Pritchard. He took over the new, purpose-built, Admiralty Signal Station, erected on the mound at the end of the point. His instructions on taking up the post were as follows:

13th June, 1805. Desire the Lieut to pay Mr Rob Beaver 2/- a Day from the 20 Sept 1804
to 17 March 1805. During the time he had charge of the Signal House.[9]

Although Beaver's workload had been reduced, by 1809 things had generally
deteriorated at the lighthouse. The pilots, expressing their concern to the Dock
Committee, reported that the light was essential for safe navigation, especially
during the winter.

This report prompted the repair of the lighthouse, including the replacement
of the two worn-out reflectors. In particular, Robert Beaver was admonished for
inattention and negligence with the recommendation that his position should
be reviewed. Two years later, it was concluded that he 'ought to be removed',
but he wasn't, possibly because of the remoteness of the posting. After another
year, the Dock Trust questioned whether it was worthwhile continuing the light.
Although the insurers felt that it might be better to close it, the pilots and ship
owners were:

> Decidedly of the opinion that the Light at the Point of Linus was highly beneficial to the
> Navigation of this Port, and therefore that it would be inexpedient to discontinue it.

In any case, it was revealed that closing the lighthouse would only save £250 a
year, so the light remained. Finally, on 30 May 1814, Robert Beaver was replaced
because he had:

> ...become so infirm (in consequence of Old Age etc) as to be nearly incapable of
> discharging the necessary duty required.

He was awarded an annuity of thirty pounds per annum out of the Docks
Charitable Fund 'in consideration of his long Service', but within a few days of
his retiring Robert Beaver died, aged sixty-five.


## A FRESH START

Beaver's replacement was Lieutenant Robert Pritchard, who became keeper on
3 June 1814. For the previous nine years, Pritchard had supervised the neighbouring
government signal station on Point Lynas. However, this duty had lately come to
an end 'in consequence of the recent Peace' and, on leaving the Royal Navy,
Lieutenant Pritchard became the ideal candidate.

His new employers obtained additional reassurance that they had the right man
for the job with:

> Several recommendations in favour of the said Lieutenant Pritchard signed by respectable
> Gentlemen in Anglesey and testimonials of his sobriety, general good character and
> fitness for the situation.

In spite of this excellent testimonial, Pritchard was required to sign a £100 bond against his removal from the lighthouse and was bound by the following comprehensive list of duties, which is the earliest set of rules issued to Liverpool lighthouse keepers.

> You are not to be absent from your duties...without receiving permission in writing
>
> You must strictly adhere to the well cleaning of the lamps, reflectors and windows...snuff and trim the lights...to ensure a strong clear light...during the whole of the night.
>
> You are to light the lamps at sunset...and continue them lighted until sunrise
>
> You are to be careful of the oil, cotton wick, tow or other articles committed to your custody that they may not be wasted, embezzled or injured...
>
> You must immediately report to the Secretary any loss or accident you may discover or observe to any Ship or Vessel in the Neighbourhood of the Lighthouse.
>
> Whenever any Accidents happen to any part of the Premises or Property belonging to the Trustees of the Lighthouse...You are immediately to report the same to the Secretary of the Trustees, and you are on no account to fail making a quarterly Return to him...

Lieutenant Pritchard's salary was fifty pounds a year, plus an allowance of five pounds for coals and candles. He was enthusiastic and active in his approach to the work. During the next two years he worked hard to improve the premises at his own expense, and his efforts were recognised by a considerable salary increase to seventy guineas (£73.50) on condition that any improvements made by Pritchard would be left after his retirement. His endeavours seem to have stimulated even grander ideas for the lighthouse. Thus, in 1816, a bill was presented to Parliament that would enable drastic alterations to be made. However, nothing was done, and it would be another nineteen years before a new lighthouse was in place.

## IMPROVEMENTS

The dangers to shipping around Anglesey's coast are very different from those encountered in Liverpool Bay. Instead of sandbanks, the major hazard off Anglesey is presented by rocky outcrops, like the Skerries, and many submerged or semi-submerged rocks, such as the notorious Cole Rock.

Over the years, the function of the lighthouse on Lynas Point was frequently reviewed. In 1818 the light was adjusted to act as a guide into Beaumaris harbour and also to help ships safely navigate down the treacherous east coast of the island. The following year a survey was commissioned by the Liverpool Ship Owners Association, which in turn prompted Trinity House to survey the area. The resulting recommendations led to the strengthening and adjustment of the light. Although it was generally agreed that the light should be moved northward, towards the end of the point, which would make it visible beyond the Skerries, it was another fifteen years before this was implemented. Helpfully, Trinity House also mentioned that they themselves 'invariably made use of the best Spermaceti Oil in their burners' because inferior oils tended to dim the reflectors with smoke. Liverpool took the hint, and from then on used the best oil at their lighthouses.

With the increase in trade, the ship owners needed to know when their vessels were approaching Liverpool. The solution was a line of signal stations from Holyhead to Liverpool. Each chosen site had to have a clear view of its neighbouring stations. The route crossed Anglesey and continued from Lynas to Ormes Head lighthouse. It then traversed the North Wales coast to reach Hilbre Island, in the Dee estuary. From here it continued to Bidston and, finally, it crossed the River Mersey to Liverpool. The Lynas station was established in 1827[10] on the hill above the Point. Each station had a tall mast on which large signalling arms were fitted, thus coded signals were sent from station to station, reporting the sighting, off Holyhead, of vessels bound for Liverpool. By 1859 the telegraph service had changed from visual sightings to an electric system. Eventually the telegraph and lighthouse services were amalgamated.

Lieutenant Pritchard's death, in 1832 at the age of fifty-eight, was reported to the Dock Committee in a letter from the Reverend John Owen, Minister of the Parish. He suggested that Mrs Pritchard was competent enough to be the next keeper, with the help of a manservant who had been there for twelve years. She had been an active participant, with her husband, in the running of the establishment. The actual physical effort involved in keeping the light required a strong arm. Mrs Pritchard was, therefore, employed as the new keeper, at the same salary as her husband, on the understanding that she continue to employ a competent assistant.

The following year an extensive survey of the 'lighting, beaconing and buoying of the approaches to the port', carried out by Captain Denham, was completed. In it, Denham concluded that the light at Point Lynas was 'most inefficient and altogether ill-calculated to answer its purpose'. Apart from being out-dated, another problem was that the light needed to be seen from the north-east quarter, 'but the high ground forming the headland made the use of the original site impossible for this purpose'.[11]

Various opinions were sought on location and design for the new light. Alan Stevenson, then in charge of the Scottish lights, suggested that a 21m (70ft) tower built on the same site would be the answer. Several other designs were submitted, including one by Jesse Hartley, Liverpool's own engineer. Hartley's first design was similar to Stevenson's. Both were tall towers, but it was Hartley's that was chosen.

Hartley was one of Liverpool's most iconic engineers. His enduring legacy can be seen in many structures around Liverpool docks, but the Albert Dock itself is his major claim to fame. Opened in 1845, it was described by the *Architects' Journal* as 'a monumental masterpiece of metal and masonry construction'[12].

*Above left:* Stevenson's suggestion.

*Above right:* Hartley's original design.

## HARTLEY'S CASTLE

At the last moment the Dock Trustees decided to reposition the light further north. This would place it on the point of the headland, thereby taking advantage of the natural elevation of the land. Jesse Hartley's new scheme was revolutionary. The fact that the building would be 128ft above high water level, with an unimpeded view, precluded the need for a tower. Instead the light room is on the ground floor, with the look-out room on the first floor. In all, the structure is only 37ft high. This idiosyncratic, fort-like structure looks fit to do battle with the ferocious elements which regularly descend upon the northern coast of Anglesey.

The Marine Surveyor was asked to draw up an estimate for the cost of the lighthouse, which worked out at £500 for the dwelling, plus £400 for the lamps and reflectors. The actual cost, however, was higher at £1,165.[13] Thirteen Argand lamps with reflectors replaced the old single reflector lamp making the light visible, in clear weather, for six or seven leagues (eighteen to twenty-one miles) from a ship's deck. At the same time, Denham's extensive improvements of the

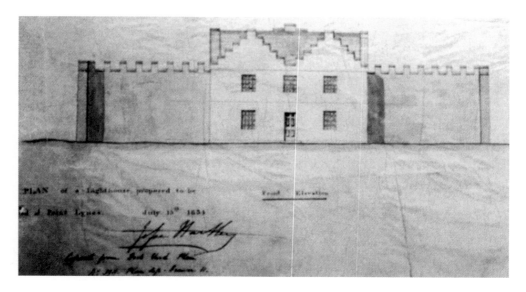

*Top:* Side elevation of Harley's new design.

*Above:* Hartley's signed 'Front' elevation, as viewed from the approach road.

*Left:* Point Lynas Lighthouse in 1840 (Viewed from the east).

approaches to the port were detailed in a *Notice to Mariners* and implemented on
1 August 1835. A major difference in the new light was that it would be effective
to seaward, rather than just 'upon the *long shore* aspect'.

In March 1836, the Dock Trust expressed concern about the second reading
of a parliamentary bill, whereby Trinity House was trying to get control of
*all* lighthouses. Liverpool did not, at this time, wish to lose their lighthouses,
but oddly enough (given that they'd just spent a large amount on the new
building) they specified that they had 'no objection to relinquish Point Lynas'.
As it turned out, however, they did not release Lynas, or any other of their
lighthouses, to the control and ownership of Trinity House.

The new lighthouse attracted the interest of the U.S. Navy, and the Marine
Surveyor was happy to give them a detailed specification:

> Marine Surveyors Office
> Septr. 19<sup>th</sup> 1838

Dear Sir

In reply to your queries (through Mr Ogden) respecting Point Elianus Lighthouse
situated at the NE extreme of Anglesea - I beg to hand you the annexed.

With sincere appreciation of your polite sentiments,

> I remain Dear Sir
> Yours very truly
> H.M. Denham

Captn Perry
&c &c &c
United States Navy

(Denham's letter to Captain Perry, U.S.N.)

Point Elianus (Lynus) Lighthouse

| | |
|---|---|
| Latitude… | 52°. 25'. 0" N |
| Longitude… | 4°. 17'.15" West of Greenwich |
| Area occupied by all the buildings including the external walls… | 1,116 yards |
| Base of Lantern above H.W. Mark (ordinary springs)… | 116ft |
| Diameter of Lantern… | 13ft 3in |
| Height of lantern | 8ft |
| Number of Reflectors… | 13 |
| Diameter of Reflectors | 22in |

Proportion of horizon illuminated...                           211 degrees

Annual Consumption of Oil...                                   596 Gallons

Can be seen from a Ships deck of 400 Tons (say Eye elevated 17ft) 18½ Miles at L.W. or 16¼ Miles at H.W.

Persons permanently appointed...                               1 Keeper at £73.10s. who finds an assistant

Annual cost of keeping it up...                                £322.8s. including the Salary and £23.0.0 for Fuel

Cost of construction & fitments...                             £2,781.8.0

Magnetic Variation                                             27° Westerly

(Signed)

H.M. Denham

(The annexe (attachment) to Denham's letter)

The figures given above differ, in some respects, from the *Notice to Mariners* which announced the opening of the light. For instance, on the *Notice* the light was said to be visible from the deck at a distance of six to seven leagues (roughly eighteen to twenty-one miles). In his letter, though, Denham states that it was only about sixteen to eighteen miles, depending on the state of the tide, and then from a height of about 17ft above the deck. According to Trinity House, the lighthouse cost £1,165 to build, but Denham gives a figure of £2,781 8s for the 'cost of construction and fitments'. Expensive fitments!

Llaneilian Parish Church.

Apart from minor repairs and painting, there were no major changes to Lynas lighthouse until 1839, when the steady light was changed to an occulting light. The new light was obscured for two in every ten seconds making it distinct from all the other lights in the vicinity. As soon as the new occulting apparatus had been installed, the energetic Captain Denham sailed to Dublin on the mail boat, 'for the purpose of observing the effect from Seaward of the flashing apparatus.' Denham also visited the lighthouse and found 'the flashing light properly fixed and working with great accuracy'. Technically however, it was not a 'flashing light', because it was lit for a longer period than it was eclipsed.

Although in the 1841 census Mrs Pritchard, the keeper was said to be fifty-five, she was actually sixty-seven years-old. Her duties at Lynas were such that she needed quite a lot of help. As well as a young male servant she also had three female servants[14]. This seems a rather large staff for one household. However, the workload had become much heavier after the installation of the occulting light mechanism.

Mrs Pritchard continued to keep the lights until she died, aged seventy-five, in 1848. As far as we know she was the oldest female keeper and one of the oldest keepers of the Liverpool lights. Between them, she and her husband had kept Lynas lighthouse for thirty-four years. During their tenure, there were no complaints about the running of the lighthouse or the quality of their service. She and Lieutenant Pritchard are buried in the peaceful graveyard of St Eilian church. The church is well worth a visit, it possesses a very finely carved rood screen with medieval paintings still visible on the woodwork, whilst the stone tower of the church dates back to the twelfth century.

## THE MORGAN FAMILY

The new keeper was David Morgan, aged thirty-four, with a salary of £84 per year. His previous post was as second keeper at the Rock lighthouse, having joined the service in 1841. Morgan was married with two children, aged seven and five. So, for the first time a young family lived at the lighthouse. Not long after they arrived, his wife Mary gave birth to a daughter and to celebrate their arrival in their new home they called her Mary Lynas Morgan. The hundred mile journey from New Brighton to Lynas would have been an arduous and expensive one, so Morgan applied for assistance and was granted £7 10s (£7.50). That may not seem much but it was a month's wages. In spite of its remoteness, this was a good posting for the young family. Instead of Mr Morgan going out on shift work, as he had at the Rock lighthouse, the family was able to be together, in their own cottage.

Generally, supplies were delivered to the lighthouse annually. This could present problems because it meant the keepers had to make sure they didn't run out of oil or basic cleaning materials. When Morgan arrived at Lynas, he set about hiring local people to do some minor maintenance jobs and also requisitioned more stores. This did not go down well with the Marine Surveyor who pointed out that Morgan was not to employ anyone without permission. Another source of irritation was the price of coal, Morgan was told that he was paying too much, more in fact than Mrs Pritchard had paid. Finally the new keeper was reprimanded for making frivolous complaints. Not a good start.

Stores for the lighthouse basically fell into three categories: lantern requirements, cleaning materials and office supplies. Sperm and olive oils, cotton waste, calico, flannel and leathers were needed for the lantern. To clean the dwelling the keeper was provided with one banister brush, one long brush, twelve birch brooms and two scrubbing brushes. Soap was also part of the stores – 30lbs of soft soap and 24lbs of hard soap; presumably for personal use, washing clothes and floors. To cope with the office side of the job the keeper received ink, blotting paper and foolscap paper. Steel pens, quills, paper and wafers (small discs of dried paste used to fasten papers together) were provided. Each lighthouse was also issued with an almanac, containing astronomical information, tide times and heights.

Two years after he arrived at the lighthouse, Morgan felt confident enough to put in a special requisition. Soon a large shipment was hauled up from the supply vessel docked at Amlwch. It consisted of a wheelbarrow, a workbench and vice along with enough tools to equip a complete workshop: a tool chest; a hammer with assorted nails, punches and a screwdriver; an assortment of saws, chisels and files; pliers, pincers and a soldering iron (with solder); a smoothing plane and an axe.

Unfortunately, the peace and quiet of Lynas was occasionally troubled by disputes with the neighbours. The local tenant at Balog Farm, Hugh Rowland,

Point Lynas on a still summer's day in 2004.

informed the keeper that he was going to close up the road which went across his fields to the lighthouse. As it was the only access road along which stores could be carried, this would have been completely unacceptable. An alternative road was proposed. Rather strangely, the person chosen to make the new road was Hugh Rowland.

Today, the approach to the lighthouse on foot from the local village Llaneilian, brings home just how isolated the situation was. A narrow road snakes up to the thick-set, sturdy tower that stands on the headland, at the end of the jutting peninsula.

Relationships didn't improve as time went on. A notice board was put up forbidding trespass. This was allegedly destroyed by the tenants at Balog farm and they were threatened with prosecution. They counterclaimed that Morgan had allowed his cattle to trespass on their land. Both parties eventually ended up in court at Chester. The keeper was told not to let his cattle roam and the farmers were warned not to trespass on the land belonging to the lighthouse. Finally, both sides seemed to settle down and no further trouble was reported.

One of David Morgan's jobs, as principal keeper, was to interview and choose new members of staff. Initially, his inexperience resulted in some questionable appointments. For instance, Philip Gibson was taken on as an assistant at 10s (50p) per week. Morgan described him as a 'sober, steady and careful man' which was probably true. Unfortunately, he overlooked the fact that Gibson 'has only the sight of one eye, which disqualifies him for the duties'.

The new recruit, John Jones, 'a good active man', was taken on in 1849. He was thirty-five years-old and lived nearby, at Pen y Cae, with his wife and five children. As the assistant keeper he received ten shillings per week. Compared to Morgan's £84 a year, Jones' salary of only £26 was very poor. After four years he applied for other employment in the service, as a labourer, saying that he was unable to support his family on his wage. It was requested that Morgan supply a report, which stated that Jones was not a seaman, but had previously only worked as a farm labourer. However, Jones was given a pay increase of 25 per cent which enabled him to stay on.

Three years later, in 1856, Jones left the service and was replaced by Lettice Morgan, the keeper's eldest daughter. She was taken on trial, as assistant keeper, at eight shillings a week. Her employer did very well out of this arrangement, paying her less than they had paid Jones ten years previously. Although she applied for an increase after a couple of years, it was denied. After another eighteen months though, her pay was increased to ten shillings a week. The modern practice of yearly wage reviews was not one adopted by the Dock Trust or its successor from 1859, the Mersey Docks & Harbour Board (MDHB). Although David Morgan applied for an increment after ten years, it was denied. In fact he never received a single wage increase in the whole of his time at Point Lynas – thirty-six years! Regular paid annual holidays were also a distant dream. Fourteen years after he became keeper, Morgan applied for two weeks leave of absence. This was granted 'on the understanding that the expense of sending an assistant to fill his place is to be borne by him'.

A *Lighthouse Commission* report of 1860 included a vivid account which sheds light on the extremely arduous working conditions endured by the keeper in operating the occulting mechanism:

> The flash is produced by boards which are turned by machinery. They turn slowly till their edges are towards the lamps and then close suddenly and shut out the light. The Machinery is wound by pulling an endless chain hand over hand rapidly. It takes the keeper 20 minutes to wind it and it goes for four hours. He says the labour is excessive – 'killing'. The wife and daughters of the keeper perform the duties of an assistant. The eldest daughter of the keeper is allowed 8/- per week. The Board [*Mersey Docks & Harbour Board*] very seldom visit the place and the machinery in particular is very rude.

In spite of these negative comments nothing was done to upgrade the machinery, or to improve the lighthouse at all for another fourteen years.

The Morgan family had to be pretty self-sufficient. Fortunately, with a large family there was always plenty of help available. When Lettice Morgan resigned, in 1863, her fourteen-year-old sister, Mary, was able to take over as assistant. The Morgans weren't the only Dock Board employees living near Llaneilian. The telegraph station was just a mile or so inland, half-way up the flanks of Mynydd Eilian. Here, improvements were introduced to the telegraph keeper's dwelling, consisting of a bakehouse, oven and a pigsty. It's possible that the lighthouse had similar 'conveniences', bearing in mind its remoteness.

David Morgan seems to have been a conscientious man – sober, steady and reliable. Even so, he was occasionally in trouble. When the *Fairfield* went down off the Anglesey coast in 1852, the cargo was cast on shore. Unfortunately, Morgan was found with some of the goods from the wrecked ship in his possession, so he had to face the magistrates. It seems that he was found guilty. However, he refuted the charge and had the backing of his employers, who, after interviewing him, stated that they 'were satisfied of the propriety of his conduct in the matter'. Furthermore, they agreed to help him out with the cost of his appeal. After that there is no further mention of the incident, so presumably Morgan's appeal was successful.

## THE INSPECTIONS

Triennial inspections were part of the responsibility of the Marine Committee of the MDHB. They would spend up to three days inspecting the lighthouses and then produce a booklet detailing their findings. In fact, the inspections covered more than just the lighthouses. The committee's brief also encompassed the telegraph stations, lifeboat stations and the lightships. Not all the reports have survived, but a typical inspection in 1864 describes the committee's activities.

Travel of course was much slower and there were fewer options for getting about, but the Marine Surveyor and the committee were able to commandeer a steam tug for their trip. Usually the inspections were undertaken in the summer to take advantage of the good weather. Unfortunately, 23 June 1864 was a poor example of a summer's day. The tug *Despatch* set off, with the intrepid Committee aboard, at 9.20 a.m. precisely. The weather couldn't have been much worse: 'the wind was blowing hard from the westward, with squalls of hail and rain and a heavy sea.' It was so bad that it was impossible to board the North-West, Crosby and Formby lightships and their inspections had to be left to another day. Instead, the tug sailed to Llandudno, where the gentlemen of Liverpool were no doubt relieved to disembark. They made their way along the coast by train, to Bangor. This was only about eighty miles from Liverpool, but it had taken them all day.

The following day they travelled to Amlwch, and then on to Point Lynas to visit the telegraph station and the lighthouse. Only minor repairs and a little painting were necessary and the condition of the premises generally, including the reflectors and the apparatus, was deemed to be in good order. However, one wonders about these inspections. On the previous one the Engineer had proposed some improvements to the winding gear. Those improvements had still not been made three years later, nor did there seem to be any urgency on the part of the Dock Board to bring the equipment up-to-date.

The report goes on to compare the salaries and conditions of the Liverpool lighthouse keepers with those employed by Trinity House and the Scottish and Irish boards. It concluded that the Liverpool keepers, on average, were paid more than their counterparts with the other boards. However, the other boards equipped their keepers with a uniform annually. The Marine Surveyor was very keen to have a similar system. He reasoned that wearing a uniform would enable the employers, 'to enforce the maintenance of a creditable personal appearance', it would give the employees pride in their employment, and it was a way of ensuring good discipline and order. As with the suggestions on upgrading the winding gear, the question of uniforms had come up in the previous inspection and, 'although favourably received had not been acted upon'. Eventually, however, uniforms were ordered at a cost of £3 each for the twelve lighthouse and the thirteen telegraph keepers.

Another aspect of the service which was mentioned in the report was the arduous nature of the job at Point Lynas. David Morgan had apparently complained that the work of winding up the machinery was unsuited for his daughter Mary, who was still only a teenager. In particular, it was very difficult for her to manage if her father was sick. The report pointed out that, 'the present arrangement has sometimes placed the service of this lighthouse in jeopardy.' In spite of this rather worrying assertion, nothing was done about the situation. Mary remained in her job and two years later, in 1867, applied for and received an increase in her wages from 10s to 12s (60p). By 1861 David and Mary Morgan had nine children, ranging in age from Lettice aged twenty to Latimer aged one. There were no servants, as in Mrs Pritchard's day, but presumably help was available from the older children.

The Morgans seem to have been reasonably content with their accommodation, but by 1875 both the living quarters and the light were giving cause for concern. A London newspaper reported: 'The light [at Point Lynas] is catoptric, of the old order, and has a range of but sixteen miles in clear weather. These are hardly conditions for a principal Light leading in and out of such a Port as the Mersey.'[15]

Another problem which had to be addressed was the lease for the land on which the lighthouse stood. As with Bidston, the landowner wanted to charge a higher rent when the lease expired. The Dock Board was not prepared to pay more, so they considered the possibility of repositioning the lighthouse further down the hill. The proposed new site was, 'not more than 320 yards from the existing lighthouse, and is within fifty yards of the site of the original lighthouse'.[16] In the end, the light didn't have to be moved as the Dock Board was able to buy about fourteen acres, including the land on which the lighthouse stood, for £2,500. At the same time, a strip of land was secured for £500, with rights of way, for a new roadway.

A sum of £4,087 was allocated for the alterations and additions. The plans were drawn up by George Lyster, chief engineer to the Dock Board, who had previously designed Orme's Head lighthouse and telegraph station. 'The Gazette' wholeheartedly agreed that it would be money well spent in view of the greatly increased trade at Liverpool:

> Point Lynas is not only a formidable headland, surrounded by outlying dangers to Shipping, but it is the limit of the cruising ground, and the rendezvous of the Liverpool Pilots. For every reason it is advisable that the Light there should be rendered quite equal to the requirements of navigation.[17]

Other changes were also implemented, including the amalgamation of the telegraph and lighthouse services. Tenders were requested for the building work, which involved new cottages and converting the existing look-out tower into a telegraph room. The firm chosen was Messrs Owen & William Thomas. Their brief was to erect two houses plus outbuildings for the keepers, and what the Dock Board called 'screen walls'. The screen walls continued the castellated theme, enhancing the building's appearance to resemble a medieval castle or fortress.

Chance Bros was the firm chosen to supply and fit a second order dioptric illuminating apparatus, complete with lantern, at a cost of £1,685. As usual, Trinity House was kept informed at all stages of the process; the improvements to the light, the changes to the exterior of the buildings, and the temporary light which had to be exhibited while the work was in progress.

After four years of reports, consultations and planning, the new houses were ready for occupation. The amalgamation of the lighthouse and telegraph station came into being in April 1879, with a complement of three men. David Morgan remained in position as the principal keeper. He was joined by Richard Roberts, who became first assistant keeper and Lewis Jones, as second assistant keeper.

*Above:* The fortress–like outline of Point Lynas Lighthouse.

*Right:* The semi-circular lantern containing its huge dioptric lens, the old Telegraph Room is above the lantern.

Both men had been keepers at the telegraph station. Morgan's wage stayed at £84 p.a., Roberts received £55 and Jones was paid a weekly wage of 15s (£39 p.a.). All the men received the usual 12 tons of coal a year and their uniform.

After many years in which the Morgan girls had assisted their father, the arrangement came to an end. Morgan's youngest daughter, twenty-four year-old Alma, who had been employed on a temporary basis, was dismissed. This was no doubt a blow, not only to Alma, but also to her father as she almost certainly would have contributed to the family budget. It was softened somewhat by a payment of £15 to the keeper for his part in superintending the building contractors. The new light was displayed on 23 April 1879 and the temporary one, which had been operating for seven months, was extinguished.

None of the men at Point Lynas received the £4 allowance which was customarily granted to other keepers in lieu of a garden. Indeed, when Roberts and Jones were telegraph keepers they were specifically excluded from this bonus following an edict from the Marine Committee:

> As to gardens at Telegraph stations, the plots already provided are scarcely worthy of mention, and, from the nature of the duties which occupy all daylight hours, it is believed that the care of a garden would offer inducement to the neglect of those duties.

In fact, the keepers were rather grudgingly granted a plot of land which was to be enclosed 'at as small an expense as possible'.

## THE LOG BOOKS

The keepers at Lynas had to keep a daily log, a large number of which have survived. The earliest cover the period 1865 – 1869; the first two books being kept by David Morgan and his daughter, Mary. On most watches, all that is written (apart from the usual Wind, Barometer and Temperature information) is '*Ormeshead light visible* [or "*obscured by mist*"] *when lights exhibited*' and '*Light, Lightroom & Machinery in Good Order*'. Occasionally, routine maintenance is recorded.

Once Roberts and Jones joined the staff, a lot more information was entered. The day's first watch used to begin at 1 a.m. Then, at 1 or 3 a.m. they sometimes entered '*snuffed the Light*' (i.e., trimmed the wick). At dawn they wrote '*Extinguished the Light.*' Normally the men on watch also stated which pilot boat was on duty, for example '*No.5 Pilot on duty and No.4 off.*' A transcription of part of the 1883 log appears opposite:

# 1883 Log of *Point Lynas Light & Telegraph*

| Day and Date | Winds Direction & Force | | Wx | Time | Remarks, Occurrences, Reports, Signals, &c., &c. | Signature of Person in Charge |
|---|---|---|---|---|---|---|
| March 29th Thurs | SSW | 7 | OV | 9am 10.30 | Ship, 3 Barques, s.s. and steamer inward. 4 miles NE No.8 Pilot Boat on duty 12 miles East No.4 & No.9. (9.5) off Lynas inward 3 miles NE J.B.C.(?) *Trevanion* Barque has a Pilot. No.8 Pilot Boat inward 10.32am | Lewis Jones |
| | SSW | 8 | OVP | Noon 2pm | Barque in tow Brig and s.s. inward 6 miles East No.4 Pilot Boat on duty and No.9 (12.10pm) No.4 Pilot Boat inward (2.10pm) | |
| | South | 8 | OM | 3pm 4pm | Ship, Barque and s.s. inward 1 mile ENE No.9 Pilot Boat on duty. (3.8pm) Off Lynas inward 3 miles NE H.V.M.G. *Patagonia* as has a Pilot. (3.58pm) | |
| | South | 9 | OMP | 6pm | Barque in tow inward. 3 s.s. outward 3miles NW No.9 Pilot Boat on Duty 6.0pm | |
| | South | 9 | OMP | 6.40 | Lights exhibited Ormeshead light obscured. | |
| | SSW | 8 | OM | 12pm | Light & machinery in good order. | |

With the arrival of Richard Roberts and Lewis Jones a new era was beginning. David Morgan wrote to his employers in 1884 stating that his health was failing and that he had become unfit for duty. The Dock Board noted that he was now sixty-nine years-old and had been in the service for forty-two years so he was 'permitted to retire' with a pension of £65 a year. He and his family had served the Board faithfully, at Point Lynas, for thirty-six years – two years longer than the Pritchards.

## REMINISCENCES OF AN OLD KEEPER

During the next seventy years or so, the routine and way of life remained much the same. Although the records for Point Lynas stretch back well over 200 years, only one personal account of a keeper has been found. Mr W.E. Schofield was interviewed in 1983 about a way of life which has vanished forever.[18]

Mr Schofield left school at fifteen and joined the Royal Navy as a signal boy. After fifteen years in the Navy, which included serving throughout the Second World War, he retired, having reached the rank of chief yeoman. Schofield began with the MDHB as a dock gateman before applying for the job of keeper at Lynas. As it was such a big change of pace, going from the frantic bustle of Liverpool to the rural isolation of Wales, Mr Schofield and his wife had to think about whether they were prepared for such a move. Eventually they decided to give it a go.

Schofield was well qualified for the job. As chief yeoman he had been trained in signalling, Morse code and semaphore. He had also been a submariner, so would have been well used to long periods of repetitive work in very trying conditions as well as working in a very tight, close-knit community. Even in the late-1940s Lynas was pretty isolated. The system of three keepers was still in force when Schofield joined. There was a principal, a junior assistant and Schofield, who became the senior assistant. Each keeper and their family occupied the three cottages within the castellated walls of what was in fact a small private estate.

Unlike the other Liverpool lighthouses, Lynas was also used as a visual signalling station for the pilots and for ships waiting for the pilot boat, which may not have been on station. The pilot boat was normally stationed two miles off-shore, and one of the duties of the keeper on watch was to communicate with the boat from the telegraph room using a Morse lamp or semaphore flags. By this means, the pilots kept in touch with their Liverpool office, the keepers sending their messages on to Liverpool via the land line telegraph, again using Morse code. Some years later, when VHF radio and a telephonic link to Liverpool were introduced, this process became much simpler.

Over the years the shift patterns changed. Mr Schofield gives two different versions of working practice. Firstly he says that it was 'three straight shifts of eight hours, three men eight hours a day, seven days a week'. However, later on he gives a different version, when he was asked, 'How were your watches arranged?' This time he answered that they used to work midnight to 6 a.m., 6a.m. to 12 noon, 12 noon to 4 p.m. and 4 p.m. to midnight. Curiously, four watches for the three keepers in a very difficult rolling shift system.

When Schofield first arrived at Point Lynas conditions were extremely primitive. There was no electricity and no running water. The water came from a rain catchment well. When this went dry, the local fire brigade filled up the sanitary tanks but the drinking water had to be obtained from 'a little well, a pump-up, in the fields' which happened to be a mile and a half away.

Working conditions were also very rudimentary. The 'incandescent paraffin light' was lit for eight seconds and obscured for two seconds in every ten. The timing mechanism for achieving this used a system similar to that of a church clock. One-and-a-half hundredweight of lead, suspended in a long metal tube, had to be hauled to the top every hour to keep the clock going. As well as this, the paraffin light needed to be pumped up at a rate of 170 pumps an hour. This left only about twenty minutes of rest in each hour. It was an arduous task. However, one advantage of the old clockwork was its reliability; it rarely broke down and needed very little maintenance. The only recurring problem was the failure of the mantles. When this happened, the light had to be shut down while a replacement mantle was fitted.

During the 1950s many improvements were introduced. Firstly, two diesel generators were installed along with a set of batteries for the light, so the primitive light obscuring system was gone forever. The electrical light was backed up with an automatic gas light plant which had its own integral occulting mechanism.

All this made a tremendous difference to the conditions of work. Later, mains electricity was added, as well as a mains water supply and in 1959 each of the three residences was fitted with a bathroom, 'complete with bath, washbasin and Calor gas water-heater'. At long last, Point Lynas lighthouse had been brought into the twentieth century.

The Marine Surveyor reported in November 1961 that 'the three keepers at Point Lynas lighthouse work a fifty-six hour week and have asked for a review of their working conditions.' He recommended that a working week of forty-two hours be adopted. This could be achieved by employing a Junior Assistant Keeper, who would live locally at Amlwch.

Eventually, the Dock Board decided to make the light fully automatic. This left Mr Schofield and his wife as keeper and assistant – a husband and wife staffing arrangement which had come full circle from the days of the Pritchards and the Morgans. But working conditions had changed out of all recognition. Old Mr Schofield unwittingly betrayed his delight at the new system:

> ...we had a time-switch put on top of the light, and when it got dusk that switched the light on, and in the morning when it got light it switched the light off. There were alarm bells fitted all over the place. We had five alarm bells for what could go wrong so all you had to do - you did not keep any watches at all - you went to bed at night just like anybody else and if the alarms went off of course everybody knew just which part of the lighthouse was alarming. If the light was alarming, or the VHF was alarming or if the fog gun was off station or all sorts of things and the lights which actually had gone wrong showed up so you knew just where to start. You did not just go up and say 'What's wrong?' - you knew what was wrong.

Mr Schofield goes on to say that when it became automatic, he and his wife could go away for brief periods and leave the light, or he could occasionally leave his wife to look after the station.

In 1973 the lighthouse was handed over to Trinity House. The Schofields were kept on and, from their point of view, the lighthouse was run more efficiently. One of the things he liked about the new regime was the twice-yearly inspection. In the past, the lighthouse had always been considered remote and the Dock Board had been stretched to look after it.

The lighthouse is still in use today, but there is no longer a keeper in charge. Instead, Trinity House has an agent, who inspects and maintains the light. The lighthouse cottages are privately owned.

# 7

# Great Ormes Head

## *Liverpool's Last Welsh Lighthouse*

*She staggered to her bearings, but the sails were new and good,*
*And the ship smelt up to windward just as though she understood.*
*As the winter's day was ending, in the entry of the night,*
*We cleared the weary headland, and passed below the light.*
Robert Louis Stevenson, 'Christmas at Sea', 1908.

Above the town of Llandudno in north Wales is the massive limestone headland known as Great Ormes Head. High up its seaward face, on a rocky promontory, a castellated stone lighthouse is perched 325ft above the sea.

Like Hoylake, Llandudno had been a small fishing village at the beginning of the nineteenth century. It became an elegant and popular Victorian watering place after the railway arrived in 1858. On the north shore, the town's fine hotels fringe the broad promenade. The graceful curve of Llandudno Bay ends with another headland, the Little Orme.

## A QUICK START

The need for a lighthouse on the coast of north Wales was first discussed in September 1861. The Marine Surveyor and the Board's Engineer, George Lyster, were asked to look for a suitable site and then to prepare and submit a plan. Within a few weeks the site had been chosen, a seventy-five year lease negotiated with the landowners (the Mostyn family), and the plans drawn up. Lyster estimated the cost of building the lighthouse at about £5,000 and the annual running cost at £380.

Jesse Hartley, the engineer who built Point Lynas lighthouse, died in 1860. His son and partner John Hartley, retired through ill-health within a year of his father's death. Seventy applicants applied for the position and George Lyster was chosen as the new Dock Engineer. With the continued prosperity of the Port of Liverpool the role of Engineer was one of great importance. In fact, Jesse Hartley had received a salary of £3,500 which made him one of the highest paid officials in the country.[1] George Lyster's challenge, when he became involved with Ormeshead lighthouse, was to live up to his illustrious predecessors. It was his first big project for the Dock Board. Whenever a new lighthouse was built, or there were any additions or changes, the Dock Board had to write to Trinity House for approval. However, the letters were more a courtesy than a request for permission. By the time the Elder Brethren replied approving the lighthouse at Ormes Head, preparations were well underway for the Board's newest undertaking. Just over a year after the start of the project notices were sent out to all the relevant authorities: the Pilots of Liverpool, the Admiralty, the Trinity Board, the Ballast Board of Dublin, and the Northern Lights Commissioners.

The lighthouse was to be lit on 1 December 1862 and advertised in all the shipping papers. The *Notice to Mariners* announced that:

> A first order dioptric fixed light will be exhibited from a new Lighthouse, situate on the Northernmost point of the Great Ormeshead, at an elevation of 325ft above the mean sea level. It will appear as a bright fixed Light when seen from any direction between the bearings NW by W ¾ W round by the North to East, and as a Red Light from East to E ¾ W.

The height of the actual building, which isn't mentioned in the notice, is 37ft. A number of different names have been used – Great Ormshead, Ormes Head or simply Ormeshead lighthouse.

Ormeshead Lighthouse. (Reproduced with the kind permission of the *Liverpool Daily Post*.)

THE TELEGRAPH STATION. LLANDUDNO

Telegraph Station on top of the Great Orme, built in 1827.

Access to the lighthouse is two miles from Llandudno pier, along the Marine Drive, a walled roadway that fits snugly into the side of the Great Orme. A walled lane branches off and leads to a gated courtyard at the lighthouse entrance.

## THE FIRST KEEPER

The first keeper of the new combined lighthouse and telegraph station was fifty-four year-old Job Jones. He had previously run the signal station on top of the Great Orme for many years. During his time at the old telegraph station, in the early part of the nineteenth century, he had become a well-known local character:

> The keeper of the station, Mr Jones, is remarkably courteous and intelligent; not only affording ready information to every inquirer, but kindly permitting visitors to watch his telegraphic operations, which at convenient opportunities he is always willing to explain; and to take a peep through his powerful telescopes at the sublime scenery of the district. A book is kept in which visitors are expected to enter their names and addresses. The solidity of the building – and it needs to be strong in such a situation – does not more readily attract the stranger's notice than the domestic comfort and cleanliness of his dwelling, which are most creditable to the industrious management of his wife

and family, every one of whom is also skilled in the use of the telegraph. A sheltered nook on the side of the hill near the station is a favourite resort with picnic parties, combining as it does, welcome facilities for the enjoyment of the glorious prospects, and of the exhilarating recreations usually characteristic of such festive occasions. And here it may be the proper place to observe, that for the accommodation of visitors, Mr and Mrs Jones have set apart a comfortably furnished room, where tea is provided on the shortest of notice, and a supply of good lemonade, soda water and other beverages of the temperance class is always to be had – refreshments which, during the summer months, are much in demand, and therefore, these arrangements at 'the Telegraph' are pretty generally appreciated.[2]

Job Jones had begun his career at Hilbre Island telegraph station in 1833. He and his wife, Susanna, had six children. Jones was well thought of by his employers, who considered him to be one of the 'steadiest and most efficient keepers of the Telegraphs'. Thus he was redeployed to the Ormeshead Signal Station (one of the principal stations) in 1842.

Initially only two keepers were named at the new lighthouse; Jones and his assistant, thirty-three year-old John Edward Hughes. A few months later Job Jones asked for an increase in the wages of a second assistant, his daughter Ellen. She had worked alongside her father at the signal station and then moved with him to the lighthouse. Over the years he was able to have her salary increased from £15 to £26.

## TEETHING TROUBLES

Although the actual light was ready on time, the residences for the keepers were not. Chance Brothers, who had installed the light, allowed one of their fitters to stay on for a month to take care of the lighthouse. This allowed Jones and Hughes to live at the old signal station, which was located at the top of the headland. Once their accommodation was finished, the keepers applied for a removal allowance. Not surprisingly Jones' request was refused as he was only moving a short distance. On the other hand, Hughes, who had relocated from Hoylake, was allowed £5. The land surrounding the lighthouse is minimal, but Job Jones applied for a shed for his cow. As the land falls away precipitously the Dock Board decided that it would not be a good idea and vetoed his request.

Things were not going smoothly at the new lighthouse as regards the building. Within three weeks of its opening, the lantern glazing was damaged by gales. Even when the damage had been repaired there were still problems. The glass chimneys were constantly breaking owing to defects in the glass, and the makers thus had to rectify the damage.

Back in 1784, twenty years after the Cheshire lights were built, there had been a major breakthrough in lighthouse technology. Aimé Argand, a Swiss engineer, invented a revolutionary new type of oil burner:

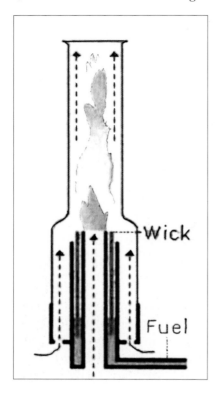

Argand Lamp, showing air-flow.

By means of a hollow cylindrical wick and a glass chimney, air was drawn up in the middle which resulted in a cleaner and much brighter flame with the wick quickly burning on both the exposed inner and outer tubular surfaces and so producing less smoke. This invention made possible the impressive multi-wick mechanical burners of the second half of the nineteenth century which might have as many as eight concentric wicks.[3]

At the beginning of the nineteenth century the principal suppliers of optics installed in lighthouses were French companies. However, from the middle of the century Chance Brothers, a British glass-maker, decided to expand their operations. To this end they built a lighthouse optics factory at Smethwick in Birmingham in 1848. Here they manufactured the framework as well as the optical lenses used in lighthouses. By the end of the nineteenth century they had 'gained a major share of supplying and installing much of the World's lighthouse equipment or optical apparatus'.[4]

Eighteen months after the lighthouse was opened the Marine Committee carried out its triennial inspection. At Ormeshead they found that all the working part of the premises; the lantern and apparatus, the telegraph office and instruments, were in 'creditable condition'. However, the living accommodation was in very poor shape. The walls on the west side of the building were so damp and the plaster so soft that it had not been possible for them to be painted and finished.

The massive dioptric lens and the telegraph room telescopes above. From the collections of the National Monuments Record of Wales: Howarth-Loomes Collection.

Before they could be decorated something needed to be done; either they should be wainscoted – a process where wooden panelling would be attached to the lower part of the wall – or they needed battening and covering with lath and plaster.

The 1867 inspection is missing, but the 1870 one mentions other problems which had occurred at the lighthouse. What was described as 'troublesome derangements of the apparatus' had recently occurred. Apparently the lantern floor had subsided, but fortunately the problem had since been successfully rectified.

## An Unusual Home & Workplace

In spite of the initial problems, Ormeshead lighthouse is a remarkable building. All Liverpool's lighthouses, except New Brighton, had a dual purpose; as well as being a place of work they were also family homes. At most of the other lighthouses the keepers lived in cottages alongside the tower, but at Ormeshead they lived inside the lighthouse building.

The 'covered yard', shown on the plan above, is a cavernous entrance hall with pitch-pine panelling stretching 6 metres (19ft) up to a gallery. Three bedrooms are symmetrically placed on each side[5]. This gallery would have given the two families who lived there a reasonable amount of privacy. Downstairs there was a very spacious kitchen and sitting room for each family.

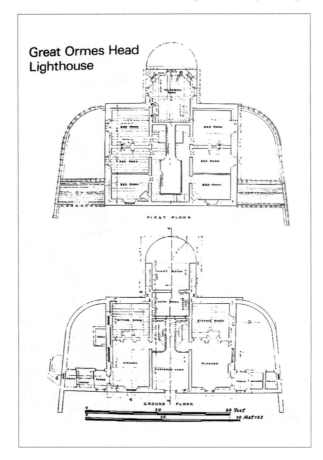

Plan of Ormeshead Lighthouse, reproduced with the kind permission of Trinity House.

All the windows were fitted with wooden shutters, so that the only visible light at sea was from the light room. Throughout the lighthouse the fixtures and fitting are of an exceptional standard. In the telegraph room there is a rack to accommodate four telescopes. Set into each window is an ingenious telescope holder which held the telescope steady, while allowing for its movement in all directions.

## THE VISITORS

The Marine Drive, which is the only access to the lighthouse, is a toll road. At first, the approach to the lighthouse was along a very precipitous route called Cust's Path. It cost one penny to use the path but it was so unnerving that the Prime Minister of the day, William Gladstone, who visited the resort in 1868, had to be blindfolded and led along the most difficult sections. The following year the Town Commissioners, presumably stung into action by Gladstone's criticism, made it a bit safer by putting railings up on the worst sections. Nine years later the path was

The 'covered yard' entrance
hall, looking towards the
light room.

replaced and the present Marine Drive was constructed.[6] The toll charges were:
pedestrians, 1d; cyclists, 2d; saddle horses, 3d and carriages, 6d [2.5p] per horse.
In 1886 instructions were given to the toll bar keepers that every person and cart
going to the lighthouse had to be charged. Fortunately, the keepers and their
families were exempt from the toll. The pedestrian toll was eventually abolished
in 1930.

   Normally lighthouses are high-profile buildings, clearly visible from both land
and sea. However, Ormeshead lighthouse is unusual because it merges into the
rocky landscape. Although the lighthouse is tucked away, half-way up the Great
Orme's north side, visitors increasingly began to seek it out. In September 1863 a
Mr Kershaw of Hull wrote to the Dock Board complaining that he was refused
admission to the lighthouse. The Board's secretary informed Kershaw that there
were simply too many visitors to the lighthouse and numbers had to be limited.
From this date a notice board was fixed at the entrance to the lighthouse that
read: '*Visitors are not admitted without an order.*' However, this did not discourage the
general public who continued, over many years, to plead with the Dock Board to
make the lighthouse more accessible.

*Left:* A telescope rack.

*Below left:* Telescope holder in a shuttered window.

*Below right:* Detail of holder.

The rise of Llandudno as a favourite, and indeed very successful, Victorian watering-place began in earnest at 8.35 a.m. on Friday, 1 October 1858, when the first train whistled, clanked and snorted out of the brand new railway station. It arrived at Conwy in less than ten minutes, where it was connected to the whole rail network: to Liverpool, Birmingham, London and all points between and beyond. Hitherto, Llandudno had been cut-off, with access only from the sea, or by the 'great hindrance'[7] of the precipitous old road.

The builders of the new line, the St George's Harbour Railway Co., also contracted a local builder, Mr Bird, to construct a landing pier. Unfortunately, no sooner was it completed than it was destroyed in the terrible storm of 1859. Nevertheless, by the time the lighthouse was built in 1862, the booming resort was crowded with visitors throughout the season. Thanks to its sheltered position, under the Great Orme and in the lee of the Snowdon mountain range, the town has a particularly mild climate.

Marine Drive, Llandudno.

The lighthouse is just two miles along Marine Drive from the castellated toll house.

## TENSION RELIEVED

At the beginning of 1882 the three keepers were Job Jones, Thomas Williams and Robert Pritchard. Everything seemed fine until half-way through the year, when Williams, the senior assistant keeper, swapped places with Joseph Trowsdale, assistant keeper at Hoylake. Salaries varied at the different lighthouses, so Williams, rather oddly, actually took a pay cut. The explanation for the transfer is hinted at in the triennial inspection report. Normally, these documents were impersonal, with the emphasis being on the state of the lighthouses rather than the personnel. Although the lighthouse was in good order, enquiries were made concerning:

> ...the accommodation provided for the junior assistant, with reference to disagreements of recent occurrence, before the exchanging of the second Keeper with the Upper Hoylake Station.

Apparently, the keepers at Ormeshead had not been getting on even though Williams had worked there for eight years without any trouble. Perhaps the 'disagreements' had something to do with the fact that Job Jones was now seventy-four and wanted a bit of peace and quiet, whereas Mr Williams had seven children, ranging in age from a toddler to a fifteen year-old. Even in this vast workplace and dwelling, Williams' many children would be much in evidence, especially in the communal areas, such as the covered yard. Mr and Mrs Williams eventually became the last keepers at Leasowe. On p.164 they are pictured in their early married life.

View of the lighthouse from the Marine Drive.

If the problem was noisy children, Jones may have been disappointed with the replacement keeper, Joseph Trowsdale, because he arrived with five children, in roughly the same age-range as the Williams' offspring. However, Trowsdale and Pritchard certainly worked well together. When Pritchard was transferred to Bidston in April 1883, Trowsdale sent a telegram to the Marine Surveyor to say that Pritchard would be in Liverpool that night and added, 'I am very sorry indeed to part with him'.

By the end of the year Pritchard, who was only twenty-six, was dead and Trowsdale died four years later aged forty-nine. Pritchard's replacement was twenty-year-old John Austin. He'd previously been a messenger at Liverpool telegraph station, so this was his first posting with the lighthouse service. Having only just arrived at Ormeshead, the keeper sent the following message to the

Marine Surveyor: 'Will you please allow slippers for Austin, he has not got any?' The answer from the surveyor is rather ambiguous, 'The slippers issued must be returned to the station'. Later that day the *Vigilant* arrived at Llandudno pier with oil for the lighthouse, *and*, presumably, the slippers.

The new Llandudno pier, opened in 1878, was a great asset to the running of the lighthouse. All lighthouse supplies were brought by sea from Liverpool, off-loaded onto carts and hauled two miles up the steep Marine Drive. This elegant pier is still in use today. Instead of the normal straight-out run, the pier has a 45° turn about a third of the way along its length.[8]

## LOG BOOKS, MESSAGES AND SHIPWRECKS

When on duty the keepers had to keep a log detailing what happened during their watch. As far as we know, the only Liverpool lighthouse log books to survive are those of Lynas and Ormeshead. A typical day's entry in the Ormeshead logs would contain the date; wind direction and force; time of entry; barometer and temperature readings, and remarks as to what was observed, such as: 'Steamers & Schooners and a Pilot boat Inward. Ship in tow Outward at 9 a.m.'. Much detail was recorded about the inward and outward-bound shipping that was observed. It wasn't always possible for the keepers to see the ships clearly, but, when they could, they named the vessels. Whilst most of the notes are routine there are sometimes more prosaic matters recorded, as in the following telegraphic exchange between the keeper and the Marine Surveyor:

Tuesday, 2nd July, 1878.
Sir, something has happened to our water pipes. We have not got any water through them since yesterday. We have opened the tank today to see if we could find anything wrong but failed to do so; there is plenty of water in it. Will you please to allow me to get a plumber at once to see what is wrong?

The Marine Surveyor's reply was succinct:

Yes – get a plumber.

Because of the remoteness of the lighthouse from the town, it has no mains water supply. Spring water is used from within the Great Orme. It flows into a coffin-like settling tank and from there into a holding tank. Nowadays the water is filtered.

Occasionally the keepers would be helpless onlookers as yet another tragedy at sea unfolded. But their reports would still be couched in the laconic jargon of the lighthouse service. 25 January 1878 started with the usual entries. The wind was force 6 NNE, the temperature 44° F. at 7 a.m. Three hours later, just before Robert Pritchard finished his watch, he noted that there was a disabled steamship (SS) 8 miles NW with '2 tugs fast to her at noon'. Thomas Williams came on watch at noon and continued to record the drama:

Mr and Mrs Williams in the family Bible.

12.00   The disabled SS is drifting to 'leeward', with her bows almost underwater, she is rolling very much and the sea going clean over her, she has just hoisted her

12.30   'Ensign', Union down at 12.30 pm.

12.40   She is now sinking and the tug backing up to her stern.

12.45   Her crew are now in the main rigging. She is nearly Hull down now and

12.56   drifting fast for the Rocks; and the 'Commander' is running up towards Beaumaris, I suppose to get the Life Boat. She has just gone out of sight round the NW corner of Puffin Island

1.00   and I think is on the Rocks at 1 pm. An SS [steam ship] at Anchor in Beaumaris has the following Signal Flying B.D.G. (A Vessel Aground) at 1.10 pm. The Beaumaris Life Boat is now in tow by one of Jolliffe's tugs standing towards the Wreck at 2.15 pm.

Wind: NNW force 8. Bar: 29.208. Ther: 47. Ship standing for

3.10   Beaumaris. P.[Pilot] Boat on duty at 3 pm. The Life Boat is now returning from the

3.20   Wreck. There seems to be none of the SS crew in the Boat at 3.15 pm.

Under the headline, 'Wreck of the steamer *Pioneer*', a local newspaper vividly reported the details of what Pritchard and Williams had witnessed as they peered through the lighthouse telescope and jotted notes into the logbook. It seems that during a raging storm the disabled *Pioneer* had been on tow, with tugs fore and aft. As the steamer and the tugs entered Penmon Sound, between Anglesey and Puffin Island, the line to one of the tugs had broken. Shortly afterwards the second line parted, leaving the stricken vessel drifting towards the rocks of Puffin Island. Apart from the tugs, the pilots also became involved. They, with two crew-members from the tug *Knight Commander*, were landed on the lee-side of Puffin Island and crossed the island to the point where they could see the steamer:

> …and found her pitched upon a bed of jutting rocks, which run out for some distance into the sea. Her hull was partly under water. The crew had taken to the rigging. At much personal risk the rescuers let themselves down by means of ropes from the steep rocks to the level beneath.[9]

During the time the men were making their way across the island, the master of the steamer had tried to swim ashore carrying a line with a lifebuoy attached. The end of the line was secured to the vessel. However, the captain was washed away and drowned. Fortunately, the rescuers managed to retrieve the end of the line and secure it. Using the lifebuoy as a breeches buoy they succeeded in saving nine of the crew;

> The carpenter, an old man, being benumbed, was unable to place himself properly in the buoy, and in consequence fell over into the sea; but the surf at the time running furiously landwards, carried him to the rocks, when he was seized by Roberts [Robert Roberts, one of the pilots]. It required *all* the strength of the rescuer to enable him to retain his hold, and had not a second come to his help, he and the carpenter would have been swept away by the receding wave. The poor man, however, did not rally, and with the captain and the second mate made up the number who was lost.[10]

With great difficulty the rescued men were helped up the rocky cliff-face to the shelter of a hut. The survivors were in:

> …a most pitiable condition, only two having shoes on their feet, the others being cut by the sharp rocks, so that a stream of blood flowed from the place where they were standing.[11]

The pilot, Robert Roberts, was a real hero, risking his life more than once to save the shipwrecked men. But others did their bit, too:

> …with singular forethought the mate of the *Nellie Mary*, who helped to man the lifeboat, placed therein a keg of rum, which undoubtedly contributed not a little to the revival of the ship-wrecked crew.[12]

Although the keepers at Ormeshead were not part of the lifeboat crew, they were sometimes involved in rescuing those at sea. During the many gales which swept the north Wales coast the keepers had a clear view of vessels in distress. Sometimes, as in the case of the *Pioneer*, they were unable to alter the course of events. On the other hand, they were more than willing to help if they could. In November 1890 John Austin did just that. With heavy seas running, and gale-force winds battering the coast the keepers realised that a ship was in trouble. Austin ran the two miles down the Marine Drive into the town and raised the alarm. The lifeboat was launched and he volunteered to go out with it. Once at sea the lifeboat was able to get alongside the ship – the Caernarfon brigantine *Planet* – and rescue the crew of five. All arrived back safely, but the *Planet*, with her cargo of coal, was lost[13].

## The Old Man Leaves

After a lifetime in the service of the Dock Board, Job Jones eventually retired in 1885. The local newspaper made much of this by featuring a comprehensive biography. Included is a rather rose-tinted view of the old man's working life, finishing with glowing good wishes:

> …the importance of the onerous duties Mr Jones has had to discharge must not be overlooked. During many a solitary night he has kept watch over his lantern, which acted as a beacon to the tempest-tossed mariner and warned him of danger…
> Mr Jones is now in the 82nd year [77th, according to the Dock Board records] of his age, and judging by the agility he displayed in walking down Mostyn Street the other morning there is every prospect of his becoming a centenarian.[14]

In fact the writer's prophecy wasn't quite fulfilled. Mr Jones was eighty-seven when he died in 1896. The *Llandudno Advertiser* carried a very fulsome account of his life and his funeral,[15] ending with the following:

IN MEMORIAM
The late Mr Job Jones, Leonard Terrace (late of Great Orme's Lighthouse).

A godly man today we laid to sleep
Hushed by the rolling of the mighty deep,
Close to the spot where he for years so brave
Trimm'd Mercy's lamp to foil the treach'rous wave,
Kind-hearted friend, serene through age and care,
Called by the Master to the mansions fair;
The pearly portals of eternal bliss
Ne'er opened to a purer soul than his.

After Job Jones retired a new, younger team of keepers took over. The principal keeper was William Mathias, a married man in his forties, who had joined the service when he was twelve years-old. Like his two fellow keepers he had been born in Cheshire; in his case on Hilbre Island. Alongside Mathias was John Austin, now promoted to second keeper, and James Dodd, who was twenty-one years-old.

Six months after Jones retired, the Marine Surveyor suggested that it might be a good idea to use paraffin instead of colza oil at Ormeshead and Point Lynas lighthouses. At Ormeshead the change would necessitate building a small oil store

Oil store and stable building, with room above, perhaps for the junior assistant keeper. The wash-house is opposite.

room costing £30, and at Point Lynas the alterations would cost £15. In addition, each station would also need four new burners for the lamps at a cost of £15 each. In total £165 would have to be spent. On the other hand, there was a potential saving in the running costs of £130 a year, so it was decided to go ahead.

Over the years various different oils had been used for the illumination of Liverpool's lighthouses. Spermaceti (whale oil) was used at the early Cheshire lights when they converted from open fires. However, by 1847 olive oil had been introduced at Liverpool, mainly as an experiment.[16] Eventually though, colza (rape seed oil) was found to be more effective as it was less sooty, produced a brighter flame and was cheaper. Unfortunately, a major drawback was that potentially dangerous fumes were generated, which could render the keeper unconscious. To counteract this hazard increased ventilation had to be introduced. Trinity House was so worried about the problem that they asked their Scientific Adviser, Michael Faraday, to redesign the lamps to provide the necessary ventilation. Presumably these modifications were adopted at the Liverpool lights as there are a number of references concerning adequate ventilation in the lantern.

Outside the lighthouse there are a range of outhouses; one building was used as an oil store and stable and, in 1893, a washhouse was built in which a 'small cooking range' was installed, at a cost of £50. This may have been for the use of the third keeper, who was always young and unmarried. As the main building was designed for two families, the small room above the stable could have been where the third keeper slept.

## A Reporter's Visit

A good, clear insight into the running of the lighthouse was given by 'Sinbad Junior' – a reporter from *The Sunday Chronicle*. By 1894, when the article was written, Mathias and Austin had been joined by Robert Eccles as the junior assistant. Having been met at Llandudno railway station 'Sinbad' described his journey to the lighthouse:

> In the gloaming we clattered – Mr Austin, the pony and I – through the quiet streets of Llandudno and upon the steep, broad way that winds around the 'Head' and leads to the lighthouse. [17]

The reporter sits and chats with the principal keeper in the lantern. The lamp itself is described thus: 'around the central glow the iridescent lenses catch the rays and throw them out into the silent night'. Mathias's account of how hard the work can be on a stormy winter's night is related in the reporter's typically Victorian prose:

> ...the whirling snow on the wings of the shrieking blast clings to the broad lattice of the light room, and the sea is thundering in the Monk's Cave 300ft beneath the spot where we sit. On such nights, when the blinding snow is frozen on the panes, the light keeper in his lonely watch must out with him through the narrow door in the solid masonry, close the portal so that no sudden relentless blast may blow in icy breath upon the light, and then, clinging to the glacial wall, make his way to the massive windows, and, climbing by the aid of the iron grips that stud the casements, go up and up to the topmost pane and clear the snow away. [18]

The previous year, 1893, the lights at Ormshead had been improved so that the fixed red and white light was altered to an occulting white and red light. It was a complicated sequence in which the light was lit for 16 seconds, followed by 2 seconds eclipsed. Then, alternately, 2 seconds lit and 2 of eclipse, three times. Therefore, in every minute the light was eclipsed for sixteen seconds. The candle power of the light was also substantially increased and the intricacies of the light were explained by the keeper, in laymen's terms, to the reporter:

> 'This light,' says the youthful Eccles, who is third hand in the crew, 'is visible to any vessel running from any direction between East-South-East and West-a-half-south. On the latter bearing it disappears.' 'When the light, shining through that long strip of red glass, disappears, it warns the mariner of his approach to the edges of the East and west Hoyle Banks. When the red is kept in sight it leads a mile to the northward of these obstructions. Vessels running up channel pick up Point Lynas – there it is winking away – and then take the Mersey Pilot.' [19]

From the workplace 'Sinbad' continued his tour of the lighthouse with the principal keeper. Later on, after a look at the keepers' accommodation, they settled down before a warm fire:

> And then the Principal Keeper, with his little nephew on his knee, tells of things he has seen in the long years he has been in the Service. Clearest of all, and most terrible of his many memories, is the loss of the *Juno*, which drove ashore on the outer edge of Taylor's Bank, close to Crosby Lighthouse.
>
> 'I saw the men as the ship struck,' said the keeper, 'Climbing into the rigging and clinging to the shrouds, until man after man was swept away. God help us all, Sir! They could see the lifeboats fairly swarming round the edge of the bank; but nothing could be done. The sea was running as I never saw it run before, and hope never again to see it. The water was too shallow for the lifeboats to get near and nothing, nothing, could be done. In a short while the masts broke and went with a lurch to leeward, carrying into the boiling surf the few poor souls that still remained; and every man perished! It was truly an awful night!' And the little boy on the keeper's knee nestles his curly head closer to his uncle's breast, and I…Well, I'm only a sorry listener to tales like this, and I go into the domicile of Austin and, with much chatter, strive to forget the fearful scene which the keeper's simple story has conjured up.[20]

With the details given in Mathias' account; the ship's name, and where she foundered, it is possible to work out when the shipwreck occurred. At that time Mathias had been a keeper at Bidston lighthouse, from which, with the aid of his powerful telescope, he would have had a clear view of the sinking. Ten years later, retelling the story to the reporter, none of the details he had witnessed had been forgotten. The only ship that fitted Mathias's description was the iron-hulled, full-rigged ship *Juno* which had set off from Liverpool on Monday 21 January 1884 for Calcutta, with a cargo of salt.

As she made her way out of the Mersey and into Liverpool Bay, the *Juno* struggled against a strong breeze as far as Moelfre Bay, Anglesey, where she took shelter for a couple of days.[21] Then she was taken under tow as far as the Skerries, where the tow rope parted. In increasing winds, she proceeded northward under sail. After that she either decided to retreat back to Liverpool, or was swept back by increasingly violent westerlies. During Saturday and Sunday a force 10 storm blew up, pushing the *Juno* onto Taylor's Bank, where the barque sank. The captain, his wife, the pilot and twenty-nine crew members including the four apprentices were all lost. Later it emerged that two stowaways had also drowned. The crew came from all over Europe and even from India. Both the New Brighton and Crosby lifeboats were launched but were unable to help any of those on the stricken ship:

> The poor fellows, who could be seen clinging to the rigging, had to be reluctantly abandoned to their cruel fate, and one by one they were swallowed up by the remorseless waters.[22]

Closing ceremony at Ormeshead lighthouse.

## THE FINAL YEARS

As the nineteenth century drew to a close many changes took place. William Mathias, who had steadfastly kept the lights, sent in his letter of resignation. He was sixty-five years-old and had been with the Dock Board for almost fifty-four years. As the son of the telegraph keeper on Hilbre Island, he had followed in his father's profession, working first at Holyhead, then at Bidston lighthouse and finally Ormeshead. He typified the type of men who worked long and hard to uphold the traditions of the lighthouse service.

In 1923 Ormeshead was converted into an 'unattended light' (i.e. automated) at the cost of £1,574 10s. Of Liverpool's lighthouses, only Point Lynas and the Rock lighthouses were still manned. Following automation, it was decided that only one keeper, R. Eccles, was needed to look after the Board's property and to carry out signalling duties. In 1965 the lantern was finally lit by electricity, with 190,000 candle power.

After 111 years as a Liverpool lighthouse, control of Ormeshead passed to Trinity House on 2 April 1973. The original lantern, from which the light first shone, on 1 December 1862, was still in use when it was finally extinguished in 1985 and is now housed in the visitor centre on the Great Orme.

In the picture above, the Principal Keeper Ken Chapman lowers the Trinity House ensign. Captain P.M. Edge, Elder Brother, is on the extreme right.

Although Trinity House ran the lighthouse, the Dock Board owned the property until 1985 when it was sold. It is now privately owned and has been converted into a splendid bed and breakfast establishment.

# Appendix A

From the minutes of *The Minute book of the Point of Air Lighthouse Trust, 1775–1889*, held at Cheshire and Chester Archives and Local Studies:

At a meeting held 17 January 1776: *Ordered that the following Estimate & Queries with their answers be entered in this book for the Inspection of the Subscribers.*

*An Estimate made by Mr Hamilton and Mr Meredith of the Expense of erecting a Lighthouse upon the same Construction as the Hoylake one, which is 52ft high, Diameter at the bottom from out to out 25ft 9in. Do. at the top 16ft.*

|  | £ | s | d |
|---|---|---|---|
| Height of the 2 Brick and half work 23ft; Diameter 24ft. Contents 189 yards (the Morter for the outside to be half Lime and the middle of the wall flushed & supposing Brick can be made near the Spot) at 6s per yard. | 56 | 14 | 0 |
| Height of two Brick work 29ft, Diameter 20ft 4in Contents 192 yards at 4s 9¾d per | 46 | 3 | 11 |
| Brick work round the Stairs height 37ft, Circumference 24ft – Contents 98 yards 6ft at 2s 3d per | 11 | 0 | 6 |
| Two Chimneys 40 yards, brick breadth, but char'd double on account of the Wings, Arches & Plaistering at 2s 3d per yd | 4 | 10 | 0 |
| Brick floor at the Bottom 42 yds at 1s | 2 | 2 | 0 |
| Twelve square yds brick length for a Coalhouse in the Inside at 2s 3d | 1 | 7 | 0 |

| | | | |
|---|---|---|---|
| Brick work about the Lamp | 0 | 12 | 0 |
| Eight Door Cases & Linteles all Deal at 12s per Seven Window Frames, Oak, 3ft square, Linteles & Boards, at the bottoms & Slides at 10s per | 3 | 10 | 0 |
| 7 windows, glaz'd with Common Glass & Journey to put them in | 2 | 18 | 0 |
| Sash frame of Oak for the Light 9ft long & 8ft high | 3 | 0 | 0 |
| Glazing Do. & Journey | 4 | 10 | 0 |
| Fifty-seven steps of Ash 7½in rise including Bearers, newel posts and making good the vacancies at 4s per | 11 | 8 | 0 |
| A Lead Sink in the Kitchen, frame, pipe thro' the Wall | 2 | 10 | 0 |
| Locks, Hinges, Latches and Catches | 1 | 0 | 0 |
| Bulk Head to close in the Stairs at the Top | 2 | 18 | 0 |
| Two partitions in the Rooms with Doors | 3 | 0 | 0 |
| Six Deal summers for 3 Floors 156ft at 1s 2d | 9 | 2 | 0 |
| Three hundred & 81ft of Deal Joyce for Do. at 2½d | 3 | 16 | 0 |
| Laying down the Beams & Joyces | 1 | 10 | 0 |
| Eight hundred 55ft of flooring Boards for Do. at 3d | 10 | 13 | 0 |
| Laying the same & Nails | 2 | 10 | 0 |
| Twenty-six yards of Flagging in the Light room & finding Plaister to bed the same in at 3s 6d | 4 | 11 | 0 |
| Plaistering and rendering the Light Room | 3 | 10 | 0 |
| Sixty-four ft of Oak summer running measure for the Roof at 1s 6d per | 4 | 16 | 0 |
| Eighty ft of Spar for Do. at 2½ & Corb for Do. 5s | 1 | 1 | 8 |
| 192ft of Oak Board for Do. to carry the Load on the Roof at 3d per ft | 2 | 8 | 0 |

| | | | |
|---|---|---|---|
| Workmanship in the Roof & Nails | 1 | 10 | 0 |
| Twenty hundred of Lead for Roof at 25s per | 25 | 0 | 0 |
| Solder for Do. | 4 | 10 | 0 |
| Lead Cistern for the Oil 3ft square, solder & Workmanship | 6 | 6 | 0 |
| Wood Frame for Do. | 0 | 10 | 0 |
| Lead Cistern for Water in the Light room & pipe to convey it from the roof thro' the Walls, solder & Workmanship | 5 | 5 | 0 |
| Six Stones for Balcony 4ft by 26ft & 5in thick very hard, come from Up: Holland working & setting the same | 7 | 16 | 0 |
| Iron Work for balcony to be railed double | 5 | 14 | 0 |
| Coping Stone round the Top | 3 | 0 | 0 |
| Painting | 3 | 0 | 0 |
| Slabbing under the foundation with Oak plank 2in thick or a Stone foundation will be much the same price | 5 | 0 | 0 |
| Copper for the Oil to feed the Lamp | 1 | 0 | 0 |
| Building a Wash house, Cow house and Necessary house larger than the Hoylake one, with a Loft for Hay etc. | 50 | 0 | 0 |
| Boatage of Timber, Lime, Lead & Flagg etc. suppose'd to be | 25 | 0 | 0 |
| B. If Brick is to be carried it will be £25 more – | | | |
| [*Total*] | 349 | 8 | 1 |

[1 shilling (**s**) = 5p; 1 penny (**d**) = 0.416666p]

*Queries made by Mr Hamilton when he went to survey the Hoylake Lighthouse which he thought necessary to answer.* [For easier reading, these questions and answers have been put into a table].

| Questions | Answers |
|---|---|
| **1** How far Mockbeggar is seen at Sea, and how far Hoylake Light? | The Mockbeggar five leagues [*about 15 miles*] and the Hoylake four, when the weather is moderately clear, if exceedingly so they may possibly be seen a league further. |
| **2** How much the diameter of each reflector? | Mockbeggar six feet Diameter and the Hoylake three. |
| **3** Why they prefer Oil to Coals and which is seen the furthest? | As the Hoylake light is to lead in one direction it could not properly be an open Coal fire, but was covered in, and Mr Hutchinson could not contrive to get the Smoak draw up an Funnell without Smoaking, and it sully'd the Glass so much as to destroy the good effect of the light, besides the Blaze was so often out and in, and wink'd and blink'd so much as to be a very unsteady light, and cou'd not be seen near so far as the Oil. |
| **4** How many lamps used in the Hoylake Light at one time and how many there are in each light? | Only one lamp 588 threads agreeable to the Sample Br't by W. Hamilton. |
| **5** How many Quarts of Oil used in one night for the Hoylake light and what kind of Oil? | Three quarts and a pint for the light and the Home use, there being generally two small lamps in the Kitchen, and the Oil is called, Spermacetty, and contracted for in London. |
| **6** How much cotton used in one wick and how much Hurds [*Twigs of willow or osier?*] | Hoylake uses about ¾ pound of Cotton, and a pound of common Hurds in one week, but the Mockbeggar uses near double that quantity. |
| **7** How much Coal it took to light it in one night when a Coal fire? | About 500$^d$ weight of Coal in one night, or rather more including the Kitchen fire. |
| **8** How the Coal light was secured from the weather? | By a wood roof with a Trunnel through the roof Leaded. |
| **9** What difference in Trouble between attending a Coal Fire and a Lamp? | The Coals are carr'd up such a height and requires such due attendance to stor, blow and feed the Fire, that one man unless he has a very active wife or a Son cannot attend it as it ought to be. |
| **10** What salary and what other allowances for attending the Hoylake light? | *Nicholas Seed* at the Hoylake Light receives £16 in Cash, £3.10.0 for Coals for the house use, and a Guinea to his wife every Christmas if no complaint. Appartments to live in, and a Stable and Shippon for Cow and Horse; if it be lighted with coals, the three pounds ten shillings is struck off, and the man takes Coals out of the common stock for House use. |

| | |
|---|---|
| **11** Whether the Mockbeggar lighthouse be of the same Construction as the Hoylake one or how different? | The same construction except about 15 yards higher. The Diameter of the Reflector three feet wider. The Cotton in the Lamp double the thickness, and consequently take double the Quantity of Oil. |
| **12** How is it possible the whole annual expence of ye Hoyle light can be £165? | The Mockbeggar and Bidston taking double the Quantity of Cotton and Oil to the Hoylake. All the four taken together may possibly be £660 expence annually, but one of the Hoylake lights cannot take near £165. |
| **13** How deep the foundation of Hoylake lighthouse and whether clay or stone? | Hoylake Lighthouse is set just below the Green Sward upon Oak slabbs, and stands exceeding well, having not the least settling in the Walls from Top to Bottom, if the foundation was deeper, it would be in the Quick sands. |
| **14** What ground Rent to Sir John Stanley for Hoylake lighthouse or whether consideration given at first? | No consideration given at first, but an annual Rent of two Guineas for the Hoylake Lighthouse. |
| **15** How much land granted round the lighthouse at Hoylake? | No land was granted round the lighthouse at Hoylake except for the outbuildings, but Bidston took in a Garden and paid a consideration of £40 at first and pays no annual Rent. |
| **16** Where the Bricks were made and where the lime and Timber came from? | The Bricks were made about two miles off, the Timber all Deal, except Roof, Stairs and Window frames, was had from Liverpoole; the lime was burn'd at Bidston Mills, and the Limestone brought from Wales. |

Mr Hamilton also supplied the following comparison of running costs between oil and coal, but there are some inconsistencies in it, e.g. 6 cwt of coal per night where earlier he had 5 cwt and the 'wages & coals' figures are different: –

Estimate of the annual Expense of the Hoylake Lighthouse made by W. Hamilton

| | £. s. d. |
|---|---|
| *Lighthouse with Oil* | |
| *320 Gall. Of Oil supposing it be bought at the best hand in London 3s 6d per Gall.* | 56. 0. 0 |
| *40 [lbs] of Spun Cotton at 2s 3d* | 4.10. 0 |
| *½ a hundred of Common Hurds* [twigs or shoots of willow?] | 0. 7. 6 |
| *Wages including Coals for the House use* | 20. 0. 0 |
| | £80.17. 6 |
| | |
| *Expences if lighted with a Coal Fire -* | |
| *Supposing 6 [cwt] of Coals per night at 5d* | 45.12. 6 |
| *Candles for the Kitchen use* | 1.10. 0 |
| *Wages and Coals for the Kitchen use* | 17. 0. 0 |
| | £64. 2. 6 |

*(From the Minute Book of the Point of Air Lighthouse Trust, 1775 – 1889)*

# Appendix B

## THE PROGRESSIVE DECLINE OF HOYLE LAKE

Each of the charts below shows the position and extent of the sandbanks, at low water, off the north-west corner of the Wirral Peninsula. The steady decline of Hoyle Lake can be seen over the 200 years covered by the charts.

**[Map 1]**

(1) In the seventeenth Century and perhaps for hundreds of years before, the lake was broad and deep, sheltered behind a huge sandbank, the Hyle or Hoyle Sand.

**[Map 2]**

(2) Towards the end of the eighteenth Century, Hoyle Sand is beginning to split into two, but the Lake is still broad and deep.

**[Map 3]**

(3) By 1840, Hoyle Sand had split into two distinct banks, the East Hoyle and the West Hoyle, with the Hilbre Swash between them. The 'Lake' had been reduced to a small creek.

**[Map 4]**

(4) At the end of the nineteenth Century, the old Hoyle Lake has disappeared completely.

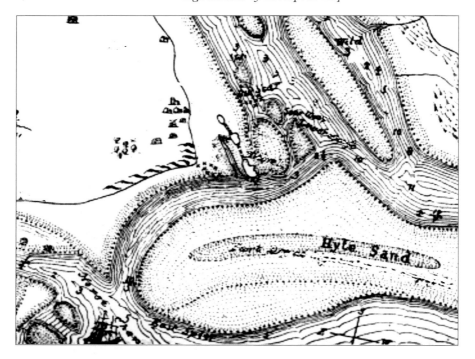

From Collins's Survey of 1689.

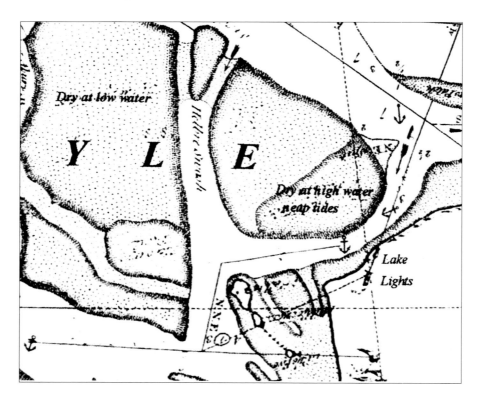

From Burdett's chart, 1771.

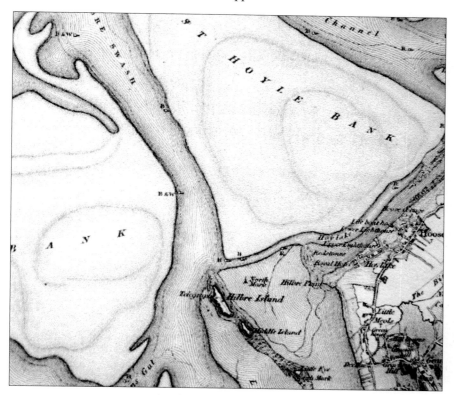

From an O.S. map, *c*.1840.

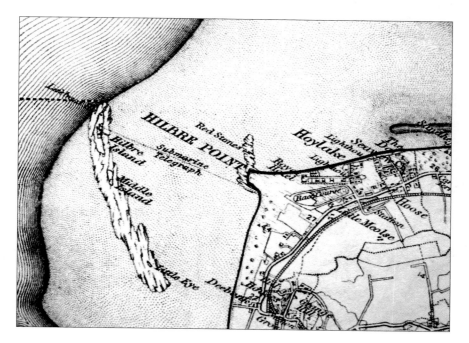

From the 1890 O.S. map.

# Primary Sources

Liverpool Record Office
Transactions of the Historical Society of Lancashire and Cheshire.
Minutes of the Dock Committee, 1793 – 1850 (352 MIN/DOC I & II)
Minutes of the Select Finance Committee, 1797 – 1865 (352 MIN/FIN I & II)
Town Books, 1738 – 1792, microfilm


Merseyside Maritime Museum
Lighthouses, Vol. I (WUP154)
Pilot Committee Meetings, 1779 – 1807 (MDHB/MP/14/1)
Extracts from Minutes of the Dock Committee, from 1699 (MDHB/1/25)
Proceedings of the MDHB, 1784 – 1945 (MDHB/MP/1, *et seq*)
*Minutes of the Marine Committee, 1855 – 1945 (MDHB/MP/13)*
*Register of Salaried Officers (MDHB/SW/1)*
*Marine Surveyor's Letter Book (MDHB/M/S)*

# End Notes

### INTRODUCTION

1. Forrester, Stanley, Birth of a Dock System in *Sea Breezes*, December, 1966.
2. Chandler, George, *Liverpool Shipping - A Short History,* (London, 1960).
3. Lacey, Louis (ed.), *The History of Liverpool From 1207 to 1907,* (Liverpool, 1907).
4. *The Tudor and Stuart Port* at www.portcities.org.uk/london (2005)
5. Sulley, Philip, *The Hundred of Wirral*, (Birkenhead, 1993).
6. Hume, A., *Outline of the Sea Coast of Cheshire* in *Transactions of Lancashire and Cheshire*, Vol. XI, p.219 (Liverpool, 1859).
7. Morris, Christopher (ed.), *The Illustrated Journeys of Celia Fiennes 1685-c1712,* (London, 1982).
8. Woods, E. Cuthbert, *Some History of the Coastwise Lights of Lancashire and Cheshire* in *Transactions of the Historic Society of Lancashire and Cheshire*, Vol. 96, p. 90, (Liverpool, 1944).
9. Hutchinson, William, *A Treatise on Seamanship*, (Liverpool, 1777).
10. Wrecks and Refugees in *Illustrated London News*, 14 August 1858.
11. Shepherd, John, 'The Problem of the Mersey Bar' in *The Bulletin*, Liverpool Nautical Research Society, Vol. 49, No 3. December, 2005.
12. Wryde, J. Saxby, *British Lighthouses – Their History & Romance*, (London, 1913).

### CHAPTER 1

1. Williamson's *Liverpool Advertiser*, 21 January 1763
2. Ormerod, George, *The History of the County Palatine and City of Chester* ed. Thomas Helsby (note by Captain Graham Hills, RN). (London, 1882).
3. Rees, J.S., 'The First and Subsequent Cheshire Lighthouses' in Transactions of the Liverpool Nautical Research Society, Vol. V, 1949-50.
4. Woods, E. Cuthbert, Some History of the Coastwise Lights in Transactions of the Historic Society of Lancashire and Cheshire, Vol. 96, 1944.
5. Hague, D.B. & Christie, Rosemary, *Lighthouses, Their Architecture, History and Archaeology*, (Llandysul, 1975).

6. Hutchinson, William, *A Treatise on Seamanship*, (Liverpool, 1777).

7. *Ibid*.

8. Stevenson, Robert, *English Lighthouse Tours, 1801*, ed. D. Alan Stevenson. (London, 1946).

9. Hume, Rev. A., *Ancient Meols*, (London, 1863).

10. Woods, E.C. and Brown, P.C., *The Rise & Progress of Wallasey*, (Birkenhead, 1960).

11. Ellison, Norman, *The Wirral Peninsula*, (London, 1955).

12. Hume, Rev. A., op. cit.

13. Beazley, F.C., Thurstaston in Cheshire (Liverpool, 1924), quotes Ronald Stewart-Brown in *The Wapentake of Wirral*: 'In 1860–1 John Baskervyle Glegg (in respect of the Hundred of Caldy), was returned in the list of Lords of the manors entitled to unclaimed wreck, his rights extending from Leighton, Dee to Seacombe (except the manors of Caldy, Wallasey and Liscard)'.

14. Ellison, Norman, op. cit.

15. *Liverpool Courier*, Encroachments of the Sea - Mutations on the Wirral Peninsula, December 29 1827.

16. *Liverpool Journal*, supplement: The Great Hurricane, 19 January 1839.

17. The following account of the Pennsylvania is given in Merchant Sail by Wm Armstrong Fairburn, published in U.S. by the Fairburn Marine Educational Foundation, (Maine, 1897): '*Pennsylvania*: 808 tons, built by Webb & Allen, New York in 1836. After less than three years service as a packet, the ship was lost in the "Liverpool Hurricane" of 9 January 1839, which also destroyed the *St Andrew* of the Red Star Line and a host of other vessels. Lloyd's estimated the marine losses from the storm at £500,000. The *Pennsylvania* was not as fortunate as the *St Andrew*, for whereas the latter packet suffered no loss of life, the *Pennsylvania* hit violently on a sandbank some three miles from shore, and of forty persons aboard, only twenty-five were saved – this being 'the heaviest toll of life in the New York packet service between 1824 and 1847'. (A British ship nearby [the *Lockwood*] suffered a loss of fifty-three persons)'.

18. *Liverpool Journal*, op. cit.

19. Holy Trinity Church, Hoylake, parish records.

20. *Liverpool Journal*, op. cit.

21. *Ibid*.

22. *Liverpool Telegraph & Shipping Gazette*, 9th October, 1850.

23. Sully, Philip, *The Hundred of Wirral*, (Birkenhead, 1993).

24. Hoylake Holy Trinity church Memorial Inscriptions, by members of Cheshire Family History Society.

25. Davidson, A.S., *Marine Art & Liverpool*, (Wolverhampton, 1986).


CHAPTER 2

1. Brooke, Richard, *Liverpool As It Was 1775 to 1800*, (Liverpool, 1853).

2. Smith, Albert, *Christopher Tadpole*, (London, 1897).

3. Proudman Oceanographic Laboratory, Insight Into Marine Science at www.pol.ac.uk, 2002.

4. Smithers, Henry, *Liverpool its commerce, statistics and institutes*, (Liverpool, 1825).

5. Findlay, A.G., *A Description & List of the Lighthouses of the World* (London, 1888).

6. Proudman Oceanographic Laboratory, op. cit.

7. Proudman Oceanographic Laboratory, op. cit.

8. Smithers, Henry, op. cit.

9. Ellison, Norman, *The Wirral Peninsula*, (London, 1955).

10. Moss, W., *The Liverpool Guide*, (Liverpool, 1796). (Reprinted 1974 by City of Liverpool Public Relations Office).

11. Bathurst, Bella, *The Lighthouse Stevensons*, (London, 2000).

12. Findlay, A.G., op. cit.
13. Stevenson, Robert, *English Lighthouse Tours, 1801*, ed. D. Alan Stevenson. (London, 1946).
14. Stevenson, Robert, op. cit.
15. *Vyner A Family History*. Privately printed – Eighty-five copies (Marylebone, 1887)
16. Woods, E. Cuthbert, 'Some History of the Coastwise Lights of Lancashire and Cheshire' in *Transactions of the Historic Society of Lancashire and Cheshire*. Volume 96. (Liverpool, 1945).
17. Dock Board Triennial Report. Astronomer's Report to the Marine Committee (Liverpool, 1864).
18. *Ibid*.
19. Boumphrey, Ian, *Birkenhead A Pictorial History*, (Chichester, 1995).
20. Smith, Albert, op. cit.

## CHAPTER 3

1. Sulley, Philip, *The Hundred of Wirral*, (Birkenhead, 1993).
2. 'Hoyle Lake' first appears as a 'place of residence' in West Kirby parish register, in 1774.
3. Fiennes, Celia, *The Journeys of Celia Fiennes*, ed. Christopher Morris, (London, 1947).
4. Roberts, Stephen J., *Hoylake and Meols Past*, (Chichester, 1992).
5. Pilot Committee Minutes, 1 April 1783.
6. Dock Trust Minutes, Report of the Committee for the Lighthouses, 17 June 1766.
7. Point of Ayr Lighthouse Trust Minutes, 1775 – 1889 held at Cheshire & Chester Archives & Local Studies, Cheshire Record Office, Chester.
8. *Ibid*.
9. Hawkes, G.I., 'The Point of Ayr Lighthouses', *Maritime Wales*, No. 9, 1985.
10. Point of Ayr Lighthouse Trust Minutes, op. cit.
11. Ormerod, George, *The History of the County Palatine and City of Chester* ed. Thomas Helsby (London, 1882).
12. *The Gentleman's* Magazine, June, 1776.
13 *Ibid*.
14. Ormerod, George, op.cit.
15. Larn, Richard & Bridget, *Shipwreck Index of the British Isles*. (London, 2000).
16. Morris, Jeff, *Hoylake & West Kirby Lifeboats 1803-2003*, (Coventry, 2003).
17. *Billinge's Liverpool Advertiser & Marine Intelligence*, 21st August, 1821.
18. Hume, Rev. A., 'Outline of the Sea Coast of Cheshire' in *Transactions of The Historic Society of Lancashire and Cheshire*, Vol. XI, p.219 (Liverpool, 1859).
19. Woods, E. Cuthbert, 'Some History of the Coastwise Lights of Lancashire and Cheshire' in *Transactions of The Historic Society of Lancashire and Cheshire*, Vol. 96, 1944. (p.85).
20. Young, H.E., *A Perambulation of the Hundred of Wirral*, (Liverpool, 1909)
21. Denham, H.M., *Sailing Directions from Point Lynas to Liverpool*, (Liverpool, 1840).
22. Sherwood, Bernard, *Memorandum Book*, Leasowe Lighthouse Archive.
23. Merseyside Railway History Group, *Railway Stations of Wirral* (Prenton, not dated.)
24. Woods, E. Cuthbert, op. cit.
25. Morris, Charles, *Cannon Hoylake, Celebrating 75 Years of Entertainment*, 1987.

## CHAPTER 4

1. Sully, Philip, *The Hundred of Wirral*, (Birkenhead, 1993).
2. St Hilary's church, Wallasey, parish registers (1813-1824).
3. Census, 1801.
4. Mortimer, W.W., *The Hundred of Wirral*, (London, 1847).
5. Miller, Anthony M. *The Inviting Shore*, (Birkenhead, 1996).
6. Brooke, Richard. *Liverpool As It Was 1775 to 1800*, (Liverpool, 2003).

7. Ellison, Norman, *The Wirral Peninsula*, (London, 1955).

8. Brooke, op. cit.

9. Ellison, op. cit.

10. Miller, Anthony M. op. cit

11. Bathurst, Bella., *The Lighthouse Stevensons*, (London, 1999).

12. *Ibid.*

13. Boumphrey, Ian & Marilyn., *Yesterday's Wirral*, No. 4, Wallasey & New Brighton (1986).

14. Marine Surveyor's Letter Book, MDHB/M/S. Memo dated 17 September 1838.

15. McCarron, Ken., *Fort Perch Rock and the Defence of the Mersey*, (Birkenhead, 1991).

16. Moss, W., *The Liverpool Guide*, (Liverpool, 1796). Reprinted by City of Liverpool Public Relations Office, 1974.

17. Davidson, *A.S. Marine Art and Liverpool*, (Wolverhampton, 1986).

18. *Liverpool Courier*, 29 January, 1883.

19. Round the Coast. An album of pictures from photographs of the chief seaside places of interest in Great Britain and Ireland, (London, 1895).

20. Jerome, Jerome K., editorial in *To-Day*, 29 December 1894.

21. *Ibid.*, 19 January 1895.

22. *Liverpool Daily Post* and *Mercury*, 20 August 1921.

23. Handscombe, David, 'Aground at New Brighton' in *The Bulletin*, The Liverpool Nautical Research Society, Vol. 49, No. 1, June, 2005.

24. Sunderland, Lin. 'The Lights of Liverpool Bay' in *Lamp 53*, Association of Lighthouse Keepers, December 2001.

CHAPTER 5

1. Rees, J.S., 'The History of the Liverpool Pilotage Service' in The Liverpool Nautical Research Society, Transactions Vol. 5, Liverpool, 1949 – 50.

2. Minutes of the Pilot Committee.

3. Yorke, Barbara & Reginald, *Britain's First Lifeboat Station* (Liverpool, 1992)

4. *Liverpool Courier*, 23 January 1836

5. Yorke, Op. cit.

6. Denham was promoted to commander in 1835 and to captain in 1846, although he was invariably referred to locally as 'captain' after his 1835 promotion.

7. Yorke, Op. cit.

8. Yorke, *Ibid.*

9. Yorke, *Ibid.*

10. *Liverpool Albion*, 14 January 1839.

11. Report of the Sub-committee, January, 1839.

12. *Ibid.*

13. *Ibid.*

14. *Liverpool Journal*, Letter to the editor, 14 January, 1839.

15. *Ibid.*

16. *Ibid.*

17. *Liverpool Albion*, 28 January 1839.

18. *Ibid.*

19. *Ibid.*

20. Little, Eddie, *The Great Storm*, (Bramhall, 2002).

21. Mountfield, A.S., 'Admiral Denham and the Approaches to the Port of Liverpool' in Transactions of the Historic Society of Lancashire & Cheshire, Vol. 105.

22. *Liverpool Albion*, op. cit.

23. Letter to Captain Denham, 1839, Merseyside Maritime Museum Archive.

24. 1851 census
25. *Ibid.*
26. *Liverpool Courier*, 3 February 1898.
27. *Liverpool Echo*, 29 March 1887.
28. Barrow, J.P., *Crosby Lighthouse*, 1955.
29. Liverpool Courier, 8 February 1898
30. *Waterloo and Crosby Herald*, 5 February 1898
31. *Ibid.*
32. *Liverpool Courier*, 3 February 1898.
33. *Ibid.*
34. *Ibid.*
35. *Ibid.*
36. *Ibid.*
37. *Illustrated London News*, 12 February 1898, p225.


CHAPTER 6

1. Minutes of the Dock Committee, 22 January, 1807.
2. Rees, J.S., The History of the Liverpool Pilotage Service in *The Liverpool Nautical Research Society, Transactions* Vol. 5, 1949 – 50.
3. Denham, H.M., *Sailing Directions from Point Lynas to Liverpool,* (Liverpool, 1840).
4. Rees, *op. cit.*
5. Minutes of the Pilot Committee, 25 September 1781.
6. Quoted in an Act of Parliament of 1819 secured by the Liverpool Dock Trustees to empower them to improve or replace their lighthouse at Point Lynas. It was finally replaced in 1835.
7. Davies, H.R., *Anglesey Antiquarian Society & Field Club*, 1924.
8. Stevenson, Robert. *English Lighthouse Tours,* (London, 1946).
9. *Lieutenants at the Signal Stations.* ADM6/55, The National Archives.
10. Large, Frank, *Faster than the Wind,* (1998).
11. Hague, Douglas B. *Lighthouses of Wales,* (Aberystwyth, 1994).
12. Hughes, Quentin. *Liverpool City of Architecture,* (Liverpool, 1999).
13. www.trinityhouse.co.uk (2005)
14. 1841 census
15. *The Gazette*, London, May 14, 1878.
16. Gittins, Edward, Letter
17. *Gazette, op. cit.*
18. From transcript of interview with W.E. Schofield recorded 23 September 1983. Copy held at Anglesey County Record Office, Llangefni, ref. WM/T.1.


CHAPTER 7

1. Jarvis, Adrian, *The Mariner's Mirror*, 1992
2. Hicklin, John, *Llandudno and its Vicinity,* (London, 1856).
3. Hague, Douglas B., *Lighthouses of Wales*, (Aberystwyth, 1994).
4. Boyle, Martin, *Lighthouses To Light Their Way*, (Southampton, 1996).
5. Llandudno Lighthouse Guesthouse brochure.
6. Jones, Ivor Wynne, *Llandudno Queen of the Welsh Resorts*, (Cardiff, 1975).
7. *Illustrated London News*, 9 October, 1858
8. www.theheritagetrail.co.uk (2005)
9. *North Wales Chronicle,* 2 February, 1878 (p.6).
10. *Ibid.*

11. *Ibid.*
12. *Ibid.*
13. Jones, Ivor Wynne, *Shipwrecks of North Wales,* (Ashbourne, 2001).
14. *Llandudno Advertiser,* 13 June 1885.
15. *Llandudno Advertiser,* 4 November, 1896.
16. Boyle, Martin, op. cit., p.23
17. *Llandudno Advertiser,* 27 July 1894. Article reproduced from original in *Sunday Chronicle.*
18. *Ibid.*
19. *Ibid.*
20. *Ibid.*
21. *Liverpool Mercury,* Tuesday, 29 January 1884.
22. *Ibid.*

# Index

If you are interested in purchasing other books published by Tempus,
or in case you have difficulty finding any Tempus books in your local bookshop,
you can also place orders directly through our website

www.tempus-publishing.com